A SPORTING GUIDE TO ETERNITY

'Yet I *am always with you; you hold me by my right hand. You guide me with your counsel, and afterward you will take me into glory.*'
PSALM 73:23-24

Connor draws on experience in both Europe and America...A devotional I would recommend for every coach in the world. God truly used Steve in providing answers to many questions that face a coach and athlete.

Coach James Rexilius

Few writers have played top class sports. Steve's experience as an athlete and theologian gives him the experience to provide you with practical and helpful daily devotionals.

Eddie Waxer

This racy book packs a punch. It is not only readable and entertaining, but it is also thought provoking and profound.

Tim Mullins, Chaplain Eton College

Should be required reading, for the Christian athlete! It cuts to the heart of professional and amateur alike.

Rick McKinley, Director – Chicago Eagles Soccer

As a businessman and 'old athlete' I applaud Steve Connor on his unique ability to apply familiar, everyday language to Biblical concepts.... Fresh and Challenging.

Jack VanDiver, Businessman & Coach

A SPORTING GUIDE TO ETERNITY

A DEVOTIONAL FOR COMPETITIVE PEOPLE

STEVE CONNOR

Christian Focus

ISBN 1-85792-746-X

© Copyright Steve Connor 2002

Published in 2002
by
Christian Focus Publications, Ltd.
Geanies House, Fearn, Tain,
Ross-shire, IV20 1TW, Great Britain.
www.christianfocus.com

Printed and bound by
Bath Press
Blantyre Ind. Estate, Glasgow,
G72 0XD, Great Britain.

Design by Alister MacInnes

CONTENTS

FINISHING WELL

To Michelle

Acknowledgments

A Christian presence in the hectic and wonderful world of sport is emerging around the world. I owe much to the dogged commitment of the many 'sports ministers' who have chosen to serve Christ in this exciting, strategic and unconventional field. Much of this book has been spawned and generated from the ideas and influences of these coaches and ministers, for which I am grateful – bigtime!

Introduction

People at the top of the sports world have coaches. Good coaches are valuable. I have rarely met a competitor who did not have a few gripes about his coach. Qualities of a good coach include understanding the big picture, clearly communicating goals and objectives, teaching strategy and technique, and keeping both the team and the individual focused. A good coach can guide the athlete to reach and harness that most cherished product – human potential.

In the first four books of the New Testament we have Jesus Christ's life documented by four unique and accurate sources. A common theme throughout the text is Christ inviting others to *'follow'* Him. Christ was a natural guide, or coach. We hear faint echoes of His desire to guide in Psalm 23, King David writes: *'He guides me in the path of righteousness, for his name's sake. Even though I walk through the valley of the shadow of death I will fear no evil'*.

This little book is for sports people (for athletes) who may be looking for a guide. Jesus guided many during His lifetime – many, but not all he invited, followed. In the past centuries many have called themselves followers of Christ. You may be surprised at how Jesus and the Bible can relate to your world. That is why I called it *A Sporting Guide to Eternity*. He has invited you — will you follow?

Most of these meditations stand by themselves as an inspirational thought for the day. There are no hard rules on how to read a book of 'devotionals', so go where you're interested. But if you are new to spiritual things or you are just examining the Christian faith, may I suggest reading the first section in sequence. It should make more sense that way!

STARTING THE RACE

'But those who hope in the Lord will renew their strength.
They will soar on wings like eagles; they will run and not
grow weary, they will walk and not be faint.'
Isaiah 40:31

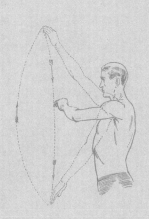

Stretching the Spiritual Muscles

When I consider your heavens, the work of your fingers, the moon and the stars, which you have set in place, what is man that you are mindful of him, the son of man that you care for him?'

PSALM 8

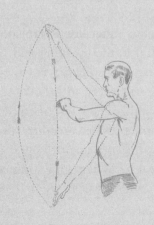

Everyone on earth has 'twenty-four' hours a day – no more, no less; they are a gift from God. The way we rush around, you would think that someone had stolen a couple of those hours. We are all trying to make the best of the hours we are given. Let me encourage you to take a bit of that time and stop, open your mind and reflect on God's power; try to understand what His glory means. I believe that you will never be able to read about, or understand God's glory as much as you can experience it. Ask God to give you that insight, ask for a peek into His magnificence.

To exercise and challenge the 'inner life' is vital to your eternal destiny. Quite often, sports people are people of the outward life, people of action. You know how to learn a skill, assimilate it, and then employ the skill instinctively in the heat of competition. This is an exciting experience that can bring pleasure and personal value. Nourishing and cultivating the 'inner life' is similar. The habit of getting up in the morning and going for a run can be difficult to form, but once developed, will exert an influence over your physical health. The habit of cultivating your very real 'inner life' is also difficult but, once formed, will exert an influence over your spiritual health. When your spiritual health is in order, your physical, mental, social and psychological well-being is consigned a healthier priority, your life will fall better into place. *(I must stop right here and give you a warning – life has many troubles, and putting your spiritual life in order is not a disinfectant to problems. Getting your spiritual life in order can give clarity and superior solutions to your problems, but probably won't result in fewer of them.)*

Training your inner life is challenging; you are busy, you may have few friends that are spiritually sympathetic and you will encounter a spiritual conflict that you may not even be aware of.

Climb the spiritual mountain and take a look towards eternity. You may not like everything you see. Take in the clean fresh air, it may hurt your spiritual lungs at first, but stretch, push and build your muscles. You may ache for a while, that is no bad thing; it means you are challenging yourself. That is life – life is eternal. You may find that many of the cravings that you like to feed on, on this earth, can be better satisfied in light of the eternal horizon.

Reflection

Nutrition is important for people in the
world of sport. Have I given much attention
to the 'inner man'?
Have I been feeding my soul?

Prayer

God in heaven help me to become aware
and attend to my inner life.

*'Our inconsistency can only be cured
by one constant.
Our infinite desire can be satisfied only by
an infinite being.'*
C.S. LEWIS

Joining the Team

'I am the way and the truth and the life. No one
comes to the Father except through me.'
JOHN 14:6

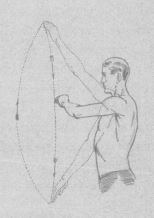

At some point in your life you decided to get involved in sport. Your mother or father may have been sporty, your brothers, sisters, and friends may have been sporty, and you may have gone to an athletic school. However, being around sport does not make you an athlete. You may have had athletic attributes e.g. a 'good balance', 'keen eye', or an 'aggressive attitude'; but until you join a team, you are not really a sports person, you are more like a fan. At a certain point in your life you made the transition from fan to participant. You signed up, tried out and were chosen for some sort of organized sport.

A few legendary sports stars grew up in remote areas of the world. As children they heard vague echoes of the sport and team they would one day compete for in distant lands. But someone noticed them and introduced them to the foreign world and seemingly strange activities they would soon outrival. Other sports stars were almost bred for sport, they gave the impression of coming out of the womb with a racquet in their hand. Some great pro's are pedigrees from second or third generation sporting heroes. Regardless of where you came from, whether it was a remote African Tribe or a famous sporting family, you made up your own mind, at some point, to join a team. You may have been pushed by an over-exuberant parent who applied too much pressure, that can be a misery. But I bet, if you are reading this, you are probably old enough to make decisions for yourself. You made a conscious effort, at some time, to join a team.

The idea of being picked for a team is not too far off the Christian life. You may have had an over-exuberant religious mum who made you go to Sunday school. You may have had religious family or friends. Perhaps you went to a religious school or live in a 'Christian' country. Or maybe you were raised in an environment (like me) remote from most things Christian. You may have peeked over the fence into that strange religious world and wondered what those people were all about; it may have seemed so foreign, so strange. You dreaded thinking about entering that religious world and the changes that may occur in your life. Yet something drew you, or is now drawing you to God. Until you make the decision for yourself – your mum, friend, husband or wife cannot make that decision – you will merely be a spectator on the sidelines. Until you say, 'Yes I want to be on God's Team (Team Jesus)', the best you can be is just a religious fan. This book is a challenge to sign-up, and to compete on Jesus' team, to build the 'inner life' and participate with Christ.

Reflection

Where am I in my Christian life? A spectator, an ardent fan, or a participant?

Prayer

Help me All Mighty God to participate in the spiritual life.

'Come follow me.'
JESUS

Why Can't We Hit the Target?

*'They have exchanged the truth of God for a lie,
and worshipped and served created things rather
than the Creator – who is forever praised. Amen.'*
ROMANS 1:25

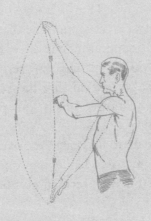

Does anybody really know what sin is any more? You do not have to prick your ears up long to get a whole load of bad definitions. One advertiser tries to entice me to buy an ice cream cone *'because it is sinfully good'*. A woman tries to rationalize gossiping behind her friend's back as, *'just a little sin'*. Bragging at a party, a friend told me he was a *'sinner'*, in the same sentence he said, *'But I don't believe in God!'*

I am rather fond of ice cream so I hope being delicious is not a sin! Good things seem to be sinful and little sins don't seem to count. So if nobody understands what sin is, no wonder we do not feel the need to rid ourselves of it. The term sin is actually an old bow and arrow expression for 'missing the target', or can be expressed as 'veering from the path'. If we do not have a target or a map for our path how can we know if we are sinning?

God gave us a target: life in perfect communion with Him. He loved us so much that He chose to communicate that love to us through His scriptures – the Bible. When God reveals himself through the scriptures, we realize that we are missing the target. And missing the target has some pretty bad consequences.

Let me try to illustrate the point. I have an old BMW motorcycle; my max speed on it is 137 mph (on the German autobahn where there are no speed restrictions, not on Scottish roads!) – pretty slow by some modern bike standards. It is a touring motorcycle designed to be comfortable for long rides. The motorcycle has an owner's manual that some German guy (probably a team of German designers) sweated over. The manual will give me a thorough guide on how to enjoy, utilize and maintain the bike. Let's say I disregard the owner's manual. Rather than using the motorcycle as a 'tourer', to travel around Europe, I use it to jump dustbins in my back lane. Perhaps I decide to drive it through rivers or rocky alpine trails. Instead of putting in petrol, I experiment with a little whisky, it has high octane and is in abundance in Scotland! As a substitute for oil I use my daughter's hair-conditioner, it promises to make things 'silky smooth'!

This is pretty far-fetched and exaggerated to make a point. What would happen to the motorcycle? It would break down! It would become, as they say in America's West Coast, 'thrashed'. The human race has disregarded God's instructions and we are paying the consequences. Try as we might in our own power, we keep missing the target.

Reflection

Try as I might in life, sometimes I really miss the target. How do I know I am going in the right direction?

Prayer

Dear God of the universe, your scriptures describe you as a Creator, Guide, Father and Good Shepherd. Do you have a design for me? Please help me to find it.

I am the Way, the Truth and the Life...
believe me when I say I am in the Father and the
Father is in me.'

JESUS

Created With A Purpose

*'For we are God's workmanship [works of art],
created in Christ to do good works, which God
prepared in advance
for us to do.'*
Ephesians 2:10

We were created *imago dei*, which means: in the image of God. We are created beings with a purpose, 'To glorify God and to enjoy him forever'. The human race was designed to be in perfect communion with God! Pick up a Bible and read Genesis 1-3; see what happened to Adam and Eve when they were *out* of communion with God. Satan lied to Eve; wretchedly, she believed a talking snake instead of God! Satan, who had been kicked out of Heaven has used the same lies ever since and they still work: *'Are you sure you want to follow God's plan for your life?' 'Won't you be more free if you disobey God?' 'He did not really mean for you to follow those rules.' 'Doing it your own way will give you a sense of self worth!' 'You do not need anybody telling you what to do! You are your own god.'* Adam and Eve fell for the lies and broke the only rule imposed on them by God. Their direct disobedience had brutal consequences: physical death, pain in child birth, submission to husband, hard work, being kicked out of a really cool garden, shame, and the worst yet – separation from God. When we disregard the rules we get 'thrashed'! I blow it in life every day because of the nature inside me; I miss the target that God has set for me.

The consequence of sin in my own life is brutal. I am hurt mentally, physically and psychologically when I veer from my original purpose. Have you ever competed when you were injured? You know you have far more potential but because some part of your body is broken you just do not have the speed or reaction. After a while you can ignore it, but you are not quite right. Have you ever driven a car with one of the cylinders not firing? You can drive it but it is not right and it will eventually hurt the engine. We are like that, we were created in God's image with great and noble purposes. When we get rid of the problem we can play better.

Reflection

It's easy to see the beautiful and the ugly in this world, but can I find both in me?

Prayer

God, it is hard to see the grime in my own life and even harder to know what to do about it. Please help me.

'For [the Christian], one essential symptom of the regenerate life is a permanent, and permanently horrified, perception of ones natural and (it seems) unalterable corruption. The true Christian's nostril is to be ever continually attentive to the inner cesspool.'
C.S. LEWIS

The Really Bad News:
We've All Got the Disease!

'Surely I was sinful at birth, sinful from the time
my mother conceived me.'
PSALM 51:5

You may only believe Adam and Eve to be an allegory for the fall of man, but there is no escaping the fact; evil is real in this world and in some degree it is in you. Most reasonable people will not object to the fact that there is a clear and present evil in our world. We see war, murder, child abuse and a bent for recklessness on the news every night. What is disagreeable is owning-up to the sin in our own lives. Our personal lying, lustful thoughts, cheating, boasting and selfishness can too easily be ignored or rationalized as character traits. To own up to our own faults can be unbearable. I hated the day after a poor game. The matches were filmed and the coach would exhibit my mistakes over and over in front of the whole team! (My coach would say: 'Good or bad, the camera doesn't lie.)

Jesus tries to explain one of his many attributes, He describes Himself as 'Light'. We all love light, unfortunately, in light we can better see the dirt. On a clear day I see how badly my windows need cleaning. Parts of society will tell you, you don't need the light, and your dirt is merely an, 'alternative lifestyle'. The scriptures quote Jesus in John 3:20, *'Everyone who does evil hates the light, and will not come into the light for fear that his deeds will be exposed.'*

As much as we try to hide or ignore them, we all live with the consequences of Adam and Eve's sin. We were designed with a purpose and when we disregard that purpose we sin. Sin denotes both an action and nature (disease). We all have the disease and it is incurable (man cannot cure it). If we are really blessed we realize that we are in a regrettable hole. But even if we recognize that we need out of this hole we unfortunately do not have the spring in our legs to jump out of it. All we can do is yell for help.

The outcome of sin is death, separation from God – Hell. I am amazed at how many will express a hope for Heaven (something they learned from the Bible) but deny the existence of Hell (also taught in the Bible). Hell, like sin, is also very misunderstood. 'I don't mind going to Hell because all my mates will be there and we can party together.' From Matthew 25:41 we see that Hell was originally for Satan and all the angels that followed him. But it will also be for all those who have rejected Christ. From the New Testament we understand those in Hell will be solitary, in discomfort, and in terror. This is bad news, but read on – it gets better!

Reflection

When I **really** look at myself in the mirror,
what do I do about what I see there?
Do I stay away from mirrors, pretend what I
do not like is not there or at least try and
ignore it?

Prayer

Lord, sometimes I try to ignore or push away
uncomfortable thoughts. Self-delusion, not
truth, is my fortress. I just do not want to
deal with certain issues! Help me to look at
my life through your perspective, help me to
rid myself of the bad inside me.

*'Someone's on the telephone desperate in his pain,
someone's on the bathroom floor doing her cocaine,
someone's got their finger on a button in some room
and you cannot tell us that we aren't gluttons for
our doom.'*
INDIGO GIRLS

Can I Impress God?

'For all have sinned and fall short of the glory of God, and are justified freely by his grace through the redemption that came by Jesus Christ.'
ROMANS 3:23-4

An NFL Coach barked at me once, 'Remember you're only around here until someone comes along who is a little stronger, faster or cheaper than you! Then you're gone!' The sober reality of professional sports is that you have to fight your way up the ranking and you only remain there until you are pushed out by someone more talented, cheaper, healthier or younger than you. To compare being 'picked for God's Team' as 'earning your salvation' or impressing God with your skills as a Christian, is poor theology. You cannot climb the ladder to attain anything in God's economy; this idea is not only dangerous, but it also stupid. We do not go up the rankings to meet God; He came down the rankings to meet us. We do not 'sign on' to God's team by impressing Him with our skill; he offers us a free ticket.

I once heard an amateur golfer desperately trying to impress a certain professional golfer with his play. The amateur was embarrassing himself with his delusional golf skills before the seasoned professional. I believe he thought the pro would not befriend him unless he was a good golfer. The pro was polite but unimpressed. So, how hard must it be to try and impress God? He is simply unimpressed with your goodness.

The Apostle Paul 'zealously' tried to impress God with his actions before his conversion. He saw Christ's followers as a threat to his cause as a Jewish leader, and even helped kill a guy because he followed Him. But God was not impressed, He was actually rather unimpressed with Paul. (God does not like it when His people are killed.) Later Paul understood the futility in trying to show-off before God. The reformed man was inspired by God to write a part of the Bible to address this very issue: trying to earn or impress your way into heaven. Here are a few small excerpts by Paul from one of his many letters in the Bible, *Romans 3:23 'For all have sinned; all fall short of God's glorious standard.' Romans 6: 23 'For the wages of sin is death, but the free gift of God is eternal life, through Christ Jesus our Lord.'*

There is nothing we can do to earn our way onto God's Team. It is a 'free gift'. Our actions and lifestyle may be impressive in comparison to some. If we compare ourselves to Hitler or the hypocrite that goes to church, we look pretty good. But when we try to make it onto God's Team by the standard of a righteous life we 'fall short'. The good news is it is a free gift. You were chosen for the team because God loves you. He values you. He even likes you and desires you to spend time with him. But you do not make the team because of your skills as a player or as a person.

Reflection

If God loves me just as I am, why do I recoil
from His love? Can I relax before God?

Prayer

Lord in Heaven, help me to respond to your
unconditional love, help me to
embrace that love.

*'Nothing you can do can make
God love you more.
Nothing you can do can make
God love you less.'*
MARK BURLINGAME

Gimme a Hand!

*'He reached down from on high and took hold of
me; he drew me out of deep waters.'*
PSALM 18:16

Lets look at a Bible story from the Gospels. In Matthew 14, Peter (one of Jesus' top guys) was out on the Sea of Galilee with his buddies. A nasty storm came up and they thought they all were going to die. Many of Jesus' friends were fishermen and boat travel was a common form of transportation, so it was not unusual for people to drown at sea. Not only was the sea raging and the passengers scared, but it also appeared that a ghost was visiting them on the water. The whole boat went into chaos. But the voice that came out of the seemingly scary phantom was reassuring. Jesus immediately said to them, 'Take courage! It is I, don't be afraid.' Peter, in an inspired moment, asked Jesus, to invite him out of the boat for a walk! Peter did well! At least for a few steps, then, '*he took his eyes off Jesus*' and started sinking! Poor Peter was truly scared! He was a tough, fisherman, I can only imagine that the storm and the experience of his first few steps on water really terrified him because he screamed, 'Jesus save me!'

Imagine how embarrassing it must have been for a seasoned sailor and career fisherman to ask for help from his leader and a non-seaman. I want my teachers and coaches to be impressed with me; failing in front of those that have influenced me most is extra bitter. If Peter was trying to impress Jesus by getting out of the boat it was a huge failure, which ended with Peter screaming for his Master's help. Peter had his pride and his own will; in the face of disaster he humbled himself and made the smart choice. Peter could have arrogantly dug in his heels and said to himself, 'If I can't save myself no one will'. I know people who think that type of self-sufficiency is dignified. Peter could have been paralysed by the disgrace of his friends watching him plead for help. Or he could have rather drowned than be indebted to his leader. But Peter chose correctly, he gasped for air and in humility, screamed for help. 'Lord save me!' All Peter's bravado, skills as a fisherman and bold talk could not save him, all he offered Jesus were the floundering hands of a drowning man. The scriptures record that Jesus 'reached out his hand and caught him.' Finally, Peter could have had second thoughts; he could have slapped the Lord's hand away and gone down. But he allows himself to be caught. His master pulls him into the boat and reminds him that he was not impressed, 'you of little faith'.

We need to put ourselves in Peter's humble position. When we realize that we are drowning and have no source within ourselves to be saved we will need someone to rescue us, we need a saviour. Ask God for the free gift of salvation through Christ. Ask God to pull you up. Reach out and take the Lord's nail-scarred hand and follow Him.

Reflection

Is there anything keeping me from asking
Christ, like Peter, to save me?

Prayer

'You hold me by your right hand. You guide
me with your counsel, and afterward you
will take me into glory.'
Psalm 73:23-24
Take my hand Lord, take my life.

*The greatness of a man's power is the measure of
his surrender.'*
WILLIAM BOOTH

Run the Race, Take Up the Mantle and Hold On Tight!

'Let us hold on unswervingly to the hope we profess, for he who promised is faithful.'
HEBREWS 10:23

The Christian life is a bit like water-skiing. Snow skiing relies on you. Water-skiing relies on the pilot of the boat. I am a horrible water-skier; I need a powerful boat to get me up. But three things I recommend about water skiing.

First, get a good pilot, one who knows where he is going and what he is doing. If you don't trust him, you are a fool. Water-skiing commits you to a pilot; you are giving him your trust, your allegiance. It is your responsibility to follow a faithful pilot when skiing.

Second, hold onto the rope! The rope is your source of power . It will pull you up and out of the water. The instructor will have given you good techniques on how to stay over the skis but if you do not hold onto the power-source you will not get very far.

Last, let go of the dock! To water-ski you must commit yourself. You need not creep along the beach watching the other skiers. Let the rope pull you out of the water and away from the land. You cannot have it both ways. Either you decide to ski or you decide you stay where you are, grasping onto the smelly dock.

How does this relate to the Christian life?

First, Jesus is like the pilot of the boat. Ask yourself if He is trustworthy. Jesus said, 'I am the way, the truth and the life, no man comes to the Father except by me'. He is saying he is the only way to get to the destination that you were designed for – Heaven and communion with God. Is he reliable or not? Allowing Christ to be the pilot or centre of your life, is scary. Jesus is not noted for his predictability. You may go places that you never dreamed of going and live with folks that you never dreamed of spending time with. Jesus says that a 'life in Him' is 'full'; nowhere does He say it is dull. Jesus says He gives us access to His Father when we hold onto Him.

Second, it is Christ's power that pulls you up, not your own. You will be pulled out of polluted water and your skill as a skier will improve, but Christ is the only source of power that will lift you out of your sin and evil. My daughter asked me for some money so she could give me a Father's Day gift. It was a joy to give her some cash – if she would of asked for more I would have given it to her. She went out and bought me a delightful little present. She was cute and so pleased to present me with a gift, but in the end the source of the gift was not her own, she had no way of purchasing the gift without my aid. I was the source of her gift. Your skill as a water-skier will improve, the tricks you will be able to execute will be fun, but if you let go of the rope, the power source – you will sink, and the water stinks.

Last, a very unpopular idea must be addressed and that is repentance. Your disease has given you some rather unfortunate predicaments. Your (please know I mean me as well) separation from God is like a mental illness. A mental illness is a disease and the disease makes you do some pretty weird things. Doing weird things does not make you mentally ill, (if so everybody at university would be mentally ill) but they seem hard to separate. Our sinful nature (disease) makes us do some pretty weird things, weird compared to the way God intended us to live. Not so weird in comparison to everyone else because the disease is common. Jesus dealt with the disease on the cross; our response is to ask Christ for help. When we decide to ask for God's help, like Peter we realize that the only way out of our predicament is Christ. Repentance actually means turning to Christ – turning away from things that we were not intended to do. Allow Christ's power to pull you away from the dock. Let God's power be your power to let go of the things that would drag you down. The more you feel God's power, and trust in His leading, the less you will desire evil. When we turn to Christ we are in the act of repenting. Hold onto Christ's power – feel Him gently pulling you out of sin and turn to Him – make this your prayer.

Why Being Sad or Sick of Our Predicament is Not Enough

'He longed to fill his stomach with the pods that the pigs were eating, but no one gave him anything. When he came to his senses, he said "How many of my father's hired men have food to spare, and here I am starving to death! I will set out and go back to my Father and say to him: Father, I have sinned against heaven and against you."'
Luke 15:16-18

When I was at University, I remember bringing a homeless person back to my house! My roommates were not impressed; he did not exactly smell like a rose. The 'street person' and I talked into the night, I realized he hated his situation! I gave him some food, clothes and shelter. The next morning I was up early and through a few connections found this chap some work and a place to stay. I was amazed that my new friend wanted nothing to do with it. He hated his circumstances but the cure (getting a job) was worse.

Sadness, or feelings of remorse, are not enough. Repentance is not hanging around feeling sorry for yourself, nor is it trying to fight off evil on your own. Repentance is turning to God; whenever you turn to God you are turning from evil, bad habits, selfishness, etc. If you think that you can throw off evil and then come to God clean, you will run out of days. It is like a chap that has cancer trying to cure himself before he goes to the Doctor. The world may try to answer sin (a spiritual cancer) with all types of cures such as: education, tolerance and self-expression. I have seen some of the most educated, tolerant and self-expressive people in the world, still locked in internal bitterness and hate.

Remember, Jesus saved Peter from

drowning – once he got into the boat he showed what kind of authority he had by calming the raging sea. He has authority over nature, he also has authority to calm the raging anger, which sits inside of man. Inside of you.

Repentance again means turning – turning to God, to His precepts and His will. It is an action that involves your emotion, intellect and will.

Reflection

Am I repulsed into action by the muck in my own life or am I stuck in it?

Prayer

Create in me a pure heart, O God, and renew a steadfast spirit within me.
Psalm 51:10

'He who desires but acts not, breeds pestilence.'
WILLIAM BLAKE

Hit the Showers

Jesus answered, "Unless I wash you, you have no part with me".'
JOHN 13:8

I knew a guy at university who went through an entire American Football season without washing his practice uniform. His jersey smelled so bad and was so discoloured by mud, grass stains and sweat that I thought it would crawl away. He never washed his training kit but at least after practice he washed himself. I have never met anyone who would walk around a whole season without taking a shower!

In Cambodia, on the Gulf of Thailand we had fun competing in a number of sports at the National Young Leaders' Christian Conference. Many of the 'young leaders' had given their lives to Christ through football/soccer outreaches. Their stories were interesting and inspiring. As the young athletes spoke I noticed the emphasis they put into one recurring theme. Over and over the Cambodian Christians mentioned that they were compelled to the Saviour who would forgive them of their sins; they had been pardoned, they were clean.

What makes Christianity so unique is that Christ has the authority to forgive sin. All other world-religions would say: do this and that and you may attain a certain level of spirituality. Jesus says, 'The Father has given me authority to forgive sin'. The remedy to this disease (sin) is not in us, we cannot shake it, no matter how good we are. But salvation comes by faith, embracing Jesus, turning to Christ (away from evil) and claiming the promises of the gospel. In this act our sins are forgiven. There is no ambiguity, no vague level of spiritual ascension. God gave us a 'covenant'; He gave us a binding legal promise. We are forgiven and our relationship to God as His children is restored through Christ.

Christ came to earth to be our sacrifice; His blood, the power of His death, will wash and break sin's power over you. That is why the cross is central to the Christian faith. It was Christ's (God's son) sacrifice on the cross that is the penalty and payment for your sin. You were bought back redeemed by the cross. This is an over-short statement of momentous truth.

Would you go your whole life without a wash? Just as your mum may not have let you come to the dinner table until you washed-up, so you cannot come to God and the incredible privileges he wants to lavish on you, unless you are spiritually clean. So access Christ's resurrected power, hit the showers – get cleaned up. You will feel like a new person.

Reflection

Am I concerned about my spiritual hygiene?
Do I know what it is like to be clean and
forgiven before my Lord?

Prayer

Lord Jesus, thank you again for dying on the
cross, I invite you to come into my life and
make me whole, make me clean.

*'Surely I was sinful at birth, sinful from the time
my mother conceived me. Surely you desire truth in
the inner parts; you teach me wisdom in the inmost
place. Cleanse me with hyssop and I shall be
clean; wash me and I shall be whiter than snow.'*
PSALM 51:5–7

He's The Boss

'Here I am! I stand at the door and knock. If anyone hears my voice and opens the door, I will come in and eat with him and he with me.'
REVELATION 3:20

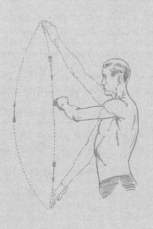

Feel your pulse beat and your blood course through your body. Grasp the fact that you not only encompass blood, bone and tissue. You also house a sophisticated psyche, a complex computer and a multiplicity of different systems: circulatory, digestive, nervous, respiratory, endocrine, immune, reproductive, lymphatic, and urinary systems. Your body has huge potential.

Another item you contain within your body is a throne. You have the capacity to host the Creator of the Universe in the core of your being, the capacity to be in the companionship of God Almighty.

A rugby player from Keble College, Oxford was the first to show me the famous portrait, 'The Light of the World', by Holman Hunt. It is a beautiful mid-nineteenth century painting of Jesus knocking at a door carrying a lantern. It was inspired by several scriptures including Revelation 3:20. The door symbolizes the entrance to a person's heart/life. The painting took three years to make and when completed was at first misunderstood. The critics laughed at Hunt and mocked that after three years of detailed work he forgot to paint a handle for the door! A friend John Ruskin boldly defended Hunt's symbolic 'Pre-Raphaelite' art in a letter to the *London Times*. In my words, the door handle is on the inside, Christ will not crash your party or force Himself into a place he is not wanted. You have to invite Him in.

When Jesus was crucified on the cross, the Temple in Israel had a thick (probably wool) curtain that separated a small exclusive part of the building. It separated the holy area from the 'Holy of Holies', which was hosting the presence of God. On Christ's death the curtain was torn, top to bottom, symbolizing that God would not be contained in a room, but now dwells inside of all who ask, inside all who were chosen. But when inviting a king into your life, be careful, He will demand centre stage, He will want to sit on the throne. Head coaches want what's best for their team, and they call the shots, so their team is unified and performs well. God wants to lead you so you will perform the best in life you can.

Reflection

I want Christ to be my Saviour but do I want
him to be my Lord?

Prayer

Father in Heaven, give me the courage to
answer your Son's calling: 'Come follow me'.

*'If anyone loves me, he will obey my teaching. My
Father will love him, and we will come to him and
make our home with him.'*

JESUS

RUN TO WIN

'Everyone who competes in the games goes into strict training. They do it to get a crown that will not last; but we do it to get a crown that will last forever.'
1 CORINTHIANS 9:25

Anxiety

'Do not fret – it leads only to evil.'
PSALM 37: 8

Psalm 37 was written for competitive people. It will help any athlete stay focused on the big picture and release them to perform better. There is a fine line between being worried and being prepared. But the line is there and to 'fret' will weaken you and take away energy that you need not release foolishly. Fretting is a warning to us that we want our own way! Do you want your way more than God's way? It is no contradiction that you can play (or live) to the best of your ability and yet desire God's will. It has been a custom around the world for years to rattle off the Lord's prayer before competition. Did you really mean, *'Thy kingdom come, thy will be done'*, or rather 'my kingdom come my will be done'?

Psalm 37:3 'Trust in the Lord and do good'. Stay under His command and focus on the task in front of you. Know that no matter where you are, you can live in the power of His love; and let God's love for you be the launching pad for your competition. Fretting leads to paralysis. In light of God's unfailing love, compete to the best of your abilities. Do all the practical things to help relieve and avoid 'fretting': pray and read your scriptures, surround yourself with like-minded friends, exercise regularly, sleep well and take in an adequate amount of nutrients. Think clearly – sometimes writing down goals, desires, pros and cons is a big help. A goal not written down is merely a wish. Remember you have a finite amount of time, so say no to the good to make time for the best.

If you desire His will and are trying to be motivated to do His will, then there is no safer place to be. You may not know where the Father's will is going to take you, but you can be sure He wants to best use the gifts and abilities He has given you.

Reflection

What ever is bugging you, write it down in a journal, and pray about it. Then go do something of service for someone else.

Prayer

Do not be anxious about anything, but in everything, by prayer and petition, with thanksgiving, present your requests to God.
Philippians 4:6

'The best stress management is: leave it at the Cross.'
JOHN SAKALA

'Anxiety does not empty tomorrow of its sorrows, but only empties today of its strength.'
C.H.SPURGEON

The Big Picture

'Let the wise listen and add to their learning, and let the discerning get guidance.'
PROVERBS 1:5

Most good coaches will ask their team: Who are we? Where are we going? How are we going to get there? Teams that have the 'Big Picture-Game Plan', a strong sense of purpose and direction, will outperform those that do not have the force of discernment. I have seen some coaches that had the small picture; they pushed their teams hard but in the wrong direction. The harder they pushed them the further away they got from their objective. Why? Because they did not have a good guide, they did not know where they were going. Teams without purpose vacillate weekly. Have you ever been lost in the car and instead of getting your bearings you just kept driving and hoping? (Okay, I write this from experience!) Unfortunately, the faster you drive, the further from your destination you go.

Being on course is great; you have a goal, purpose and destination. Living your life on course is one of those things you take for granted, until you go astray. Scripture is your map; it will point your life true north. Even the godliest man/woman needs to check their compass from time to time and make sure they are on course spiritually. In fact it is harder for an older Christian to check their direction than for a new one. A new Christian may be drastically off-course and it is blatantly obvious. But an old Christian may be pretty close to being on-line. However, there may be a few old issues, like religious pride, or cloistered greed that they have not worked through. They look like they are on course compared to some poor chap that is new in the faith. We all get complacent until we look at the game-plan. Don't be satisfied with being seven or eight degrees off course. A close look will quickly tell you that you are headed into dangerous seas. Check your map; look closely at your direction, ask the Lord to point you in the right direction. After all you may well have a whole team following you!

Reflection
Take time to get your bearings.

Prayer
Father, thanks for your guidance. Help me
to follow it.

*'Since God is synonymous with truth, in choosing to
submit to God we are submitting to a truth higher
than ourselves.'*
M. SCOTT. PECK

Beauty

'And God saw all that he had made, and it was very good.'
GENESIS 1:31

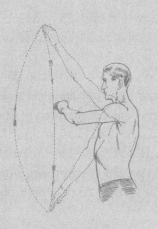

Sport can express or reflect certain qualities and virtues that are Godly. God gave us an intrinsic desire to appreciate. In sport we have a lot to admire. This may be a faint echo of our Maker: *'And God saw that it was good'*. I believe sport is art. Art can be good and bad – good when we ascribe the qualities properly, bad when we worship the activity rather than the creator. From the Christian perspective an athlete can imitate and radiate God's qualities. The origin of beauty starts with God, it's what he does. You need not be a Christian to express these qualities, but a Christian can better understand the origin of these virtues and channel the appreciation accordingly. The sports world is a tool to reach people for Christ but it is so much more; even the execution and admiration of sport is a means to glorify the Maker.

On the second day of her gymnastics class, my youngest daughter warmed up with cartwheels. She had watched her older sister at home and did her best. The cartwheels were executed poorly in comparison with the more experienced girls, but she was so beautiful in her earnest heartfelt attempt to complete the work. I knew she was trying, and it was beautiful. If an Olympic gymnast came in, her skill would pale by comparison, but her beauty would still shine. As I contemplated this, I started to look at the other girls through God's eyes, and attempted to see the scene from His vantage – the beauty was amazing. The laughter became musical, the interaction between girls was merriment, the mistakes were comical and the skill was profound. I felt as if all my senses were enhanced and I could not wait to share it with my wife. The hour and a half flew by and I wanted to look at everything this way. God gave us so many things to appreciate, enjoy and attribute His glory to.

Reflection

God is the origin of beauty; find it in your sport.

Prayer

Father thank you that my canvas to glorify your beauty is in sport.

'And wherever, in anything God has made, in the glory of it, be it sky or flower or human face, we see the glory of God.'
GEORGE MACDONALD

Body

'Do you not know that your body is a temple of the Holy Spirit, who is in you, whom you have received from God?'
1 CORINTHIANS 6:19

My friend and new Christian quit smoking after years of struggling with such a difficult addiction. He exclaimed that it was not that hard to quit, because now Christ was in his heart he did not want to blow smoke in God's face. When Jesus was crucified, the curtain in the Temple in Jerusalem was torn. God had a special presence in the Temple, in a room called the 'Holy of Holies'. The curtain dividing the room was torn top to bottom to signify that God was to fulfil His promise and change His residency. His new home is in the hearts of believers when we invite the third person of the Trinity, the Holy Spirit to pierce our body and reside in the very core of our existence. Christ's death provides the antidote for sin. When we invite Christ into our lives we join a special team and receive a King's inheritance (we were bought with a King's ransom). But with the new inheritance, come new responsibilities.

Jesus promised his poor lonely disciples that He would be with them 'Always until the very end of the age'. There is a very practical reason for God being present in us in the form of the Holy Spirit. If Jesus decided to stay in bodily form as one man you would not get close to Him. Imagine lining up to see Jesus. Perhaps because he is so busy you could only see Him for one minute. The disciples spent three years with Jesus and they still blew it, but you are happy to see him for a brief sixty seconds. You wait for your turn; unfortunately, there are six billion people on the planet and they all, for one reason or another, want to meet Him. Remember Jesus does not care about rank or how clever you are, He wants to see you too! You get in line and wait and wait and wait. Unfortunately, you really need to use the facilities, so you get out of line and dash to the toilet. A big angel on crowd-control sees you return to the line, mistakes you as a queue-jumper, and throws you to the end of the line. What a bad deal, you are the last person in the world that gets to see Jesus! Add it up! Add up six billion, times one minute! You are going to have to wait 11,500 years just to see Jesus for one minute! That is a lot of waiting around!

Fortunately, we can breath easy; He is here with you now as you read this book. He promises to never leave you and He will never forsake you. We do not have to wait around merely to get a glimpse of the super star; the super star wants to have an intimate friendship with you. You have access to God through a gift God gives you in the form of the third person of the Trinity – the Holy Spirit. He is with you now – you never need to walk alone.

Reflection

Work hard at reminding yourself Christ has
decided to take up residence in you.

Prayer

Lord Jesus, help me to play and live in the
zone of your presence.

'But I tell you the truth:
It is for your good that I am going away.
Unless I go away, the Counsellor will not come to
you; but if I go, I will send him to you.'
JOHN 16:7

Challenges

'Therefore we do not lose heart. Though outwardly we are wasting away, yet inwardly we are being renewed day by day.'
2 CORINTHIANS 4:16

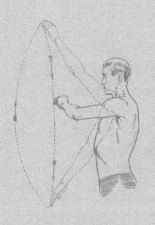

taleness is the first sign of decay. Avoiding getting stuck in a rut is a key to any training schedule. All training regimes get old unless changes are made. The body plateaus and needs a new stimulus or it won't improve. All exercise routines need variety. Your muscles get used to certain stimuli – no matter how hard you work, you need change.

Spiritually we need to be challenged or we go stale. There is nothing spiritual about sitting in the same pew for thirty years! Recently I asked a man who ran a retreat centre if he had seen any other Christian Centres lately? He replied with an air of conceit that, 'he had been too busy ministering and had not seen any other centre in ten years!' His centre had that sad stale smell.

Occasionally you encounter an old saint whose faith is vibrant and who is still being spiritually pushed. They are a great encouragement and their desire to move up a level spiritually is infectious. Recently I was sent an encouraging note by my wife's Grandpa, he is ninety-six, and he sent me the note on e-mail! It made me want to encourage others!

When is the last time you drank up God's presence with delight! Change your routine for a couple of days, pray standing up, use a different bible version or better yet use a children's bible for a week. (I dare you to take it to church and open it up for the sermon!)

Ask yourself the following questions:
- Did I really pray today (listen to God) or was I just going through the motions.
- Have I been in the Old Testament lately? Many commentaries help.
- When is the last time I memorized scripture?
- Take one proverb and incorporate it into three specifics in your daily routine.
    - For example: Proverbs 16: 32 'Better a patient man than a warrior'.
    - See yourself being patient in three specific circumstances today.

(Note: I know you stop and let God work in you or you would unlikely be reading this now, so maximise your spiritual work-out – stay focused and be renewed.)

Reflection

He is fresh every morning! Is my spiritual routine as fresh?

Prayer

Lord Jesus thank you for putting new challenges in my life that help me to focus my reliance on you.

'I love to see my friends happy, but better still – challenged.'
MARK SCHMITT

Change your Form

'And pray for us, too, that God may open a door for our message, so that we may proclaim the mystery of Christ, for which I am in chains. Pray that I may proclaim it clearly as I should.'
COLOSSIANS 4:3-4

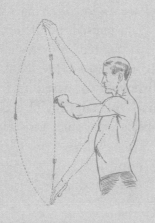

Good coaches can sustain the big picture while being flexible enough to adapt the team's strategy. Can we help the church do the same?

One summer morning I found myself in the vestry (back room) of an ancient Scottish Church waiting to preach at a 'special evangelistic service'. Sitting next to me was the old 'Beadle' (church caretaker) preparing himself to lead the processional (me) to the sanctuary! I was already a bit disheartened after peeking at the congregation – it was a sea of grey hair; not a young person in sight! I thought, 'my father in-law would love this place because it would make him feel young!'

I asked the Beadle, 'How long have you served this church?' He paused, pondered, protruded his lower lip, squinted his eyes, shook his head and said, 'Eh, just over thirty years.' I replied, 'Wow, over thirty years, you must have seen a lot of changes here!' The old man again paused, pondered, protruded his lower lip, squinted his eyes, shook his head and replied matter-of-factly, 'No!'. After the service, I thought to myself that if that old Beadle had served that church for two hundred years he would not have seen any change!

Two components of Christianity get confused: *message* and *method.*

The message must be biblically based and convey spiritual truth: The Gospel is the good news to those who put their faith and trust in the resurrected son of God, Jesus Christ. This message must never, ever change or be watered down. To dilute the Gospel is to dilute its power.

However the method is different, and open to change. There is no biblical mandate for sharing our faith. You may proclaim Christ formally and informally in a variety of ways. You can proclaim the Gospel through speech, word, picture, song, and drama... as long as biblical reliability and compassion are upheld. There is nothing sacred about the method. When one style of transmitting the method becomes more important than the message, your traditions are more important than the people outside the church.

If a coach or business person had the same results as many of our churches they would have a team of sports people who had not changed their style in generations. Imagine golfing with wooden shaft clubs, high jumping into a sandpit, sprinting on cinders, pole-vaulting with a wooden pole. If that does not hit home, how about living without penicillin or smallpox inoculations.

Reflection

Do we value sitting in comfortable pews more than making disciples? Hold tight to the message not the method.

Prayer

Father, help me to understand the difference between truth and style.

'Disregard the immaterial.'
BLAKE'S DICTUM

Cheating

*But God did say, "You must not eat from the tree
that is in the middle of the garden, and you must
not touch it or you will die." "You will not surely
die", the serpent said to the woman.'*
GENESIS 3:3

A n 'All Pro' NFL veteran told me, 'I don't cheat because I want to feel good about myself'. This is an athlete that understands what will truly satisfy. Coaches that last, understand that there are boundaries to adhere to, and that long-term victories are the sweetest.

Satan is a liar. His lies are 'subtle and crafty'. That means that his lies will take hold of you gently and strategically. He can make extremely hazardous actions seem sensible and appealing. Satan convinced Eve that instead of receiving disaster for disobeying God she would receive a reward!

Disobedience to God has never been advantageous in the broader sense. No one is saying that sin will not tantalize and entertain for a while; Satan's strategy has not changed, but if we follow him blindly it will lead to the grave. Are you aware of the consequences of sin? Do you need a reminder of what happened to Adam and Eve when their allegiance shifted from the will of the Father to their own will? The list is staggering and depressing: alienation from God, eternal damnation, aversion to good, innocent suffering, future generations of judgment, moral and spiritual blindness, guilt...

When you are tempted to cheat, free yourself by fleeing to God. When there is dissatisfaction in your life, know that Satan will lie to you, and steer you away from any solution. Evil paths lead to horrid consequences. The root word for orphan is comfortless. Jesus said in John 14 he would not leave you an *'Orphan'*, He will not leave you comfortless. Christ will alleviate any dissatisfaction – you will find truth, comfort, and eternal success in Him.

Reflection

Resolve in your will that adhering to the rules will make you a long-term winner.

Prayer

Holy Spirit convict me, make me sick, when I wilfully break God's rules.

'Injustice anywhere is a threat to justice everywhere.'
MARTIN LUTHER KING JR.

Commitment

'Whatever you do, work at it with all your heart, as working for the Lord, not for men.'
COLOSSIANS 3:23

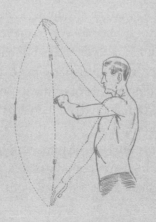

'Whatever' includes how we train, perform, and respond to team-mates and competitors. Our Christianity is not just for Sunday morning. Commitment is the ability to adhere your inner and outer self to certain principles or people you value. Scripture says where your treasure is, you will find your heart – your values. If you treasure (value) pleasing God more than men, you are committed to Him. Committing your life to Christ is not easy, but when you value Christ more than anything, you will make a healthy impact on your friends.

In a pro Bible study I attended recently I was happy to hear of one footballer (soccer player) bragging at the example his team-mate was to him. Strangely his team-mate did not quote scripture nor was he seen to be praying. It was simply his unvarying manner in the locker-room. Win or lose he was consistent. Apparently he showed respect for 'all' his team-mates, he was early for training, admitted when he was wrong but moved on, never lingering in self-pity. He said very little, but had the inner confidence that Christians have when they know God is in control of their sport and life. The team soon figured out there was something different about him.

Locker rooms can be pretty ungodly places, but retreating from ungodly places is no good. We are called to be salt and light and show

Christian principles in all areas of our life, especially our relationships. When you occupy an area of life with Christian principals, you can turn around institutions from within. No-one every said commitment was easy, but it is powerful.

Reflection

When we see through Jesus' eyes, we love
our neighbours and want to do our best.

Prayer

Father, thank you that your love will keep
me focused on your ways.

*'Darkness cannot drive out darkness, only light can
do that. Hate cannot drive out hate;
only love can do that.'*
MARTIN LUTHER KING, JR

Commitment

'Again, the Kingdom of God is like a merchant looking for fine pearls. When he found one of great value, he went away and sold everything he had and bought it.'
MATTHEW 13: 45-46

Jesus keeps trying to explain how his Father lavishes his love on us!

Even though I understand grace, my first impulse is to try to buy my way to heaven. At first glance I treat the parable of the pearl like I was taught to treat life – to be self-sufficient. In the world of sport we were taught that if we had a dream to play for a certain team, or run a certain distance, we should set a goal for ourselves and go for it. 'Sell-out' for the dream. When you find that great goal – go for it! So I equate my goal setting to my spiritual life and 'sell-out' for God! But if I am brutally honest, I have to admit that I don't have much to sell! I fail too often; I can't *really* afford the pearl. We will never be able to afford the pearl – we just don't have the cash. Fortunately, God's economy is different to ours.

Why can't you buy this pearl? Because you are the pearl! Jesus is talking about you. Do you understand your value in God's eyes? Do you see that you are so important to God that He 'lavished his love on you' and sent His son to die for you. There is no escaping it; you are valued beyond any stretch of your imagination. We can scarcely comprehend that God would sacrifice His son to purchase (redeem) that which He values so much. Consider that the creator of the universe would allow His son to be beaten and cursed by his creation so that you could be redeemed! Look back at the verse and where you see God is like a merchant looking for fine pearls, replace pearls with your name. It becomes clear you are valued beyond what you can imagine.

Understanding God's commitment to you and the value placed on your life should bring you to your knees in gratitude, ready to give yourself completely to the purchaser.

Reflection

'Sell out' for the Lord because He gave His life for you.

Prayer

Lord, I have heard so many times that you died on the cross for me; help me to appreciate its meaning.

'In him we have redemption through his blood, the forgiveness of sins, in accordance with the riches of God's grace that he lavished on us with all wisdom and understanding.'
EPHESIANS 1: 7-8

Competition

'But if you harbour bitter envy and selfish ambition in your hearts, do not boast about it or deny the truth. Such 'wisdom' does not come down from heaven but is earthly, un-spiritual, of the devil.'
JAMES 3:14-15

Characteristics of the world's best sports people are: self-control, discipline, teamwork, an ability to focus and perform under pressure, intensity, teachability and knowing how to win with grace. So how is it that when someone has a temper tantrum, gives a cheap shot, cries and moans, cheats, will not acknowledge a victorious opponent and screams at a referee, it is rationalized as being competitive! In a church meeting recently I met a man in his late thirties, he was bragging about being kicked off all the church sports teams. He assumed we would all be impressed at his machismo. He faintly conceded that he was, 'too competitive'. I had to disagree with him and suggested that he was not 'competitive' enough. Rather he was indulging in selfish ambition, disrespect, envy and lack of self-control. In other words, he was being a jackass and a servant to evil. He needed to grow up. I have a theory that it is the people who are insecure about their athletic performance who say :'if I can't play like a pro I can at least swear like one.'

The Latin word for competition means 'strive together' – to push and test an opponent to make them the best at their sport that they can be because they are being challenged. No one is implying that the stronger you are in your Christian faith, the weaker you are in your sport. The idea of 'because I am a Christian I should be a doormat and lose', generally comes from the non-sporting sector of the church who have a poor understanding of competition. Non-athletes rarely understand that the better the opponent, the better the competition. You cannot strive together if you are a doormat. You cannot compete well unless you give the best of your talent, a maximum effort.

You would ask no less of a Christian surgeon. So be competitive, make the best use of your God-given abilities for His glory. It's a God thing.

Reflection

I was asked by a pencil necked Professor in a psych class: 'How does one condone playing the violent game of American football; a game that is associated with violence, injury and occasionally death, and call oneself a Christian? I replied, 'I hit them with all the love I've got!'

Prayer

Lord, in all I do let it glorify you.

'Competition is the sincerest expression of holiness. We have God-given talents, and are fully expected to use them whenever we play.'
VINCE LOMBARDI

Confidence and Conceit

'Let us not become conceited, provoking and envying each other.'
GALATIANS 5: 26

Two quick ways to ruin a team – create a culture of conceit and envy.

Conceit is not confidence and envy kills unity. Conceit is an exaggerated, distorted view of self, which can create paralysis. Confidence is courage, trust, boldness and it produces freedom. To acknowledge that you have talent is not conceit. Maximizing your talents and improving your weaknesses is healthy. The difference between conceit and confidence is vast, but on the surface it may not appear to be different. You are confident when you have a realistic view of your skill, you understand where these talents come from and you utilize them. Conceit is a self-exaggerated view of self, which leads to self-centredness, delusion and a false sense of superior importance. A conceited person has a non-connective-ness – without an independent reality their world becomes small. When conceit grips you, and your achievements do not measure up to the assessment of your abilities, envy and blame creep in and cause disunity. Conceit stunts development. You no longer have the aspiration to listen to sources of correction and instruction.

Envy is cultivated by mere extrinsic appraisal! Sport, academics and church-life, sadly, all foster this attitude. You are spiritual because you sing well, you are smart because you got a good grade, and you are great because you jump the best. Your value is interpreted by comparison. No account has been made for your internal value measured by God. That is why we are encouraged not to judge others. I remember playing poorly after my Father died. My coach stuck with me – he was not merely a statistics keeper. He actually told me that 'under your circumstances you are playing fantastically'! That was what I needed to release me to play at the next level. Understand the big picture, it will keep you from conceit and envy! God created you with intention: 'to glorify God and enjoy Him forever'. When you use, develop and enjoy your God-given gifts and talents for God and His glory you will feel His confidence.

Reflection

Evaluate your worth by God's value set on you, on the cross.

Prayer

Gracious Father: Thank you again and again that you really think I am fun to be around.

'I may be the best in the world, but I am only jumping into a sand pit.'
JONATHAN EDWARDS – TRIPLE JUMPER

'God sends nobody away empty except those that are full of themselves.'
D.L. MOODY

CORPORATE POWER

Joshua told the people,
"Consecrate yourselves, for tomorrow the Lord will
do amazing things among you.""
JOSHUA 3:5

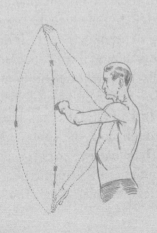

Have you ever been part of a team that is firing on all cylinders? Good performance and unity are inseparable. All teams work collectively and corporately. There is no 'I' in team, but there is an 'I' in win! Joshua knew from past failures how to motivate his army. A unified team develops commitment to a common purpose, momentum, synergy and loyalty. The more united the team, the better they play. The better the team plays the more the individual feels a sense of accomplishment. Individuals are extensions of the team. The better you perform the better your team-mate will look. A student of sport will understand better than a casual fan how individuals perform well because of the right complementary combination of team-mates around them.

At first glance, Joshua's rally call seems to be for individuals to do 'amazing things', but I am struck by the words 'among you', indicating a corporate power. It does not say do amazing things, 'in you', but 'among you'. Westerners are pretty caught up in individual fulfilment. Self-expression, self-worth, self-esteem and personal-bests are common catchwords in both the sports and business worlds. These narcissistic pop-culture themes can permeate the church like a cancer. Nevertheless, 'no man is an island', especially within the family of God. There is no scripture that suggests you should go to a church that will 'meet your spiritual needs', yet this is sadly a common criteria for finding a church.

God created you with purpose and a unique set of skills to use in His body. There is more than one club in a golfer's bag. Discover where you are useful and how you fit into the game-plan. When you are all working towards the same goal it is exciting what the Lord will do 'among you'.

Reflection

Are you pleased when a friend succeeds? Do you cheer when a Christian does something special?

Prayer

'We will shout for joy when you are victorious and will lift up our banners in the name of our God.'
Psalm 20:5

'Weak things united become strong.'
FREDERICK DOUGLAS

Courage and Cowardice

'One of the criminals who hung there hurled
insults at him: "Aren't you the Christ? Save
yourself and us!" But the other criminal rebuked
him, "Don't you fear God," he said, "since you are
under the same sentence? We are punished justly for
we are getting what our deeds deserve. But this
man has done nothing wrong." Then he said,
"Jesus remember me when you come into your
kingdom. Jesus answered him, I tell you the truth,
today you will be with me in paradise."
LUKE 23:40-41

Cowardice, *n.* *'Lack of courage to face truth, difficulty, danger and opposition.'*

Judas was a terrible coward. If he could have understood the depth of Christ's power and willingness to forgive him, he could have been saved. Jesus has forgiven many cowards, betrayers and traitors since Judas; the gospels record that all Jesus' closest friends fled, or denied they knew him. Judas was a mysterious chap; when Jesus suggested that one of his closest would betray him while they were eating supper, the apostles did not turn to Judas and say, 'Oh we know who the swine is!' Judas was given many responsibilities, but any good motives he had were now misguided by envy, selfish ambition and greed. Jesus appealed to Judas several times – Jesus could foresee the betrayal, but it did not mean that Judas could not have avoided his traitorous act. Judas traded in his dream of a Kingdom with Jesus for a little cash.

Courage, n. 'The quality of mind that enables one to encounter difficulties and danger with firmness'. Jesus models courage: the ability to adjust to specific concerns while sustaining a fidelity to the big picture i.e., God's will. Judas hangs himself in a field on the same day Christ is hanging from a cross. In contrast, Judas was completely self-absorbed and Jesus was exhibiting complete disregard for His own will.

Jesus is fulfilling the great purpose of God, being the ransom for sin, being the cure for the problem of evil. He is being crucified, nails in hands, sword through side, gasping for air, being taunted, and worse – knowing He will feel the separation from his Father. Yet even while He is fulfilling destiny, Jesus characteristically shows concern for the individual; the common thief next to him on the cross and the welfare of His mother at His feet.

When I was working with sports people at Oxford University I invited them to hear an evangelist from London. The students would probably only give me one opportunity to invite them to something. The speaker had an unsophisticated accent yet he had a sterling reputation. J. John looked around at the students packed into the hall and exclaimed, 'Oy, you think you're so smart!' My reaction was terror, as he seemed out of sync with the students. But fear quickly changed to confidence as he continued. 'You think you are so smart, you follow Kant, Nietzsche, Machiavelli, Shelly, Russell! Where are they now! I'll tell ya – they're dead! I follow somebody who's alive! You're going down a road and you come up to a fork in the road. You see five dead blokes laid out. You see one guy alive; who are you going to ask directions from? Who are you going to follow?'

Follow courage – follow Christ.

Reflection
God gave you the greatest model of courage
in His son Jesus.

Prayer
Lord of Heaven I believe you can make me
strong and courageous.

*'To this you were called, because Christ suffered for
you, leaving you an example that you should follow
in His steps.'*
1 PETER 2:21

Creativity

'Be imitators of God, therefore, as dearly loved children and live a life of love, just as Christ loved us and gave himself up for us as a fragrant offering and sacrifice to God.'

EPHESIANS 5:1-2

Arguably, we all have an innate desire to be creative. The mere fact that we are alive substantiates my point. If that were not so why are their over six billion people on the planet? We love to create. This is visibly true with children – there is an instinctive craving to draw, paint and sculpt. Watch little kids of any culture with a crayon in their hand. It is an enjoyable and profoundly satisfying experience to observe this little act of spontaneous creative combustion. It is best to watch little-ones who have not yet been inflicted with the curse of self-consciousness and comparison. Recently I received a letter that my mother wrote to her mother, it extolled my intrinsic aptitude for art! I cannot draw stick men! My mum did admit that I sketched her with horns and my father was wearing a skirt! I cringe at what the amateur pop psychologist will interpret there! But I loved art and I was no exception. Creating is a universal longing.

Sport can be a beautiful form of creativity. We long to 'make' that great play. Every season coaches create a new team, new style, and new form. If you stop creating you get in a losing rut. Creativity is expensive. You must pay for it in thought, energy, nerve and time. Routine is an energy saving device but not a favourable environment for creativity.

So why do we enjoy creating? Could it be we get it from our father, our Heavenly father?

Genesis 1:27

'So God created man in his own image, in the image of God he created him.'

Remember, our Lord is not finished with you!

Reflection

Imitate your Father and offer it back to Him as praise. That is what glorifying God in sport is all about!

Prayer

Creator of the Universe thank you for creating me. Please help me to radiate your creativity.

'Creation is the activity of an artist possessed by the vision of perfection; who, by means of the raw material with which he works, tries to give more and more perfect expression to his idea, his inspiration or his love. From this point of view each human spirit is an unfinished product, on which the Creative Spirit is always at work.'
EVELYN UNDERHILL

Evaluation

'Therefore no one will be declared righteous in His (God's) sight by observing the law; rather, through the law we become conscious of sin.'
ROMANS 3: 20

An old lady went into her Doctor's office and said, 'I am breaking wind terribly, but the good news is it does not stink nor can anyone hear it. In fact, I have been breaking wind in the waiting room for twenty minutes, but of course you would not have known it.' The Doctor gave her some medicine and said, 'see me next week'. The old lady came into the his office a week later incensed saying, 'those pills you gave me were useless, in fact they were counter productive; I still break wind, but now they stink!' The Doctor seemed pleased saying, 'that's a good sign, now that your sinus's have cleared up I can give you something for your hearing'!

The Apostle Paul after years of trying to follow the Mosaic Laws realised that the Law's function was to make you aware of how desperately you needed a saviour and how badly you stink. In Romans, Paul is reminding us that the 'Law' – God's sanctioned institution – is the standard we don't live up to. It is a measuring rod for honesty and it quickly shows our shortcomings. Most sports have their own fitness test as a way to assess your physical condition. It is a moment of truth, am I in condition or not? In the NFL you may be tested by running the forty yard dash and bench pressing 225 pounds as many times as you can. In rugby and soccer they often use a 'bleep test', running twenty metres between two bleeps that get sequentially faster to judge your stamina. You may not like the truth, but a fitness test is very revealing. You and your coach will know where you are strong and where you come up wanting. God's law is a fitness test none of us pass. It is a useful tool to remind us of our great need for a Saviour. Unfortunately, God's fitness test opens our sinuses!

Reflection

Light is helpful to direct the way and to show you the dirt.

Prayer

Father I do not want to sleepwalk through life. Help me to see your reality and respond.

'Everyone of the twenty-five years I have spent as a club manager has been a learning experience.'
SIR ALEX FERGUSON

Evaluation

'Above all else, guard your heart for it is the well-spring of life.'
PROVERBS 4:23

I f you are an athlete of any description you know you have to train hard to be any good.

Everyone is more capable in one area of their sport than others. Most of sport is taken up in training, where you assess and develop your skills. You may know people whose talent seems to come effortlessly; but to be at the top, you need to exert a lot of effort. A great sports person measures their skills and works hard to improve both their strengths and weaknesses. Maybe you are strong but slow, you have great hand-eye co-ordination but you are too cautious. You have good upper-body strength but you are prone to leg injuries. Athletes push themselves meticulously because they have a goal and desire to accomplish it.

The writer of Proverbs reminds us that we also need to diligently cultivate our spiritual life. Many athletes can push themselves physically but don't consider working-out spiritually. Our spiritual life needs maintenance. Have you assessed your spiritual health lately? Paul encourages you to take a sober look at your life, how are you doing?

Diligently look over your spiritual life with the eye of a good coach and set some spiritual goals for yourself. You may have a goal to run sixty miles a week or train all the major muscle groups once a week. Goals that are not written down are merely a wish. Spiritual discipline is the same: assess how you are doing, perhaps you should ask your local clergy (spiritual coach) for help; then write down some goals.

Reflection

This week did I…

- Study my bible
- Pray
- Enjoy other Christians' company
- Share my faith

Prayer

Help me to enjoy the process and product of your training.

'Aim at nothing and you will hit it.'
COACHES' DICTUM

'If you do what you have always done and think what you have always thought, there's a good chance you will get what you've always got.'
TIM HANSEL

Evaluation

'For the sinful nature desires what is contrary to the Spirit and the Spirit what is contrary to the sinful nature... But the fruit of the Spirit is love, joy, peace, patience, kindness, goodness, faithfulness, gentleness and self-control. Against such things there is no law. Those who belong to Christ Jesus have crucified the sinful nature with its passions and desires. Since we live by the Spirit let us keep in step with the Spirit.'
GALATIANS 5:17, 22-25

Have you ever had a coach try to improve your form, change your grip, widen your stance or modify your position? Often in the heat of battle you will revert back to old comfortable habits. The technique is not very good but you are comfortable with it. You may have gotten away with it when you were young, but to stay in the Premier League you have to work on new skills and better form, especially in the heat of competition.

Have you asked Christ to fill you with the Holy Spirit? Do you acknowledge that Christ has now made His home in your heart (the very core of your being) and wants to help you live up to your potential? Do you recognize that Christ leads you as if He were walking next to you? These are some of the Holy Spirit's attributes. It is a power that is sometimes very uncomfortable, but change usually is awkward at first.

Many times as Christians we slip back into the 'old form', out of habit. We have either not considered nailing it to the cross, or in times of stress we feel more comfortable in our old life, which does not make it in God's 'Premier League'. Good coaching produces good form, which produces results! Paul calls the 'results' of the Holy Spirit 'fruit'. God wants us to have good results from His coaching – good fruit! 'God Results'.

Here are a few excerpts taken from a Bible study of professional sports people. How can you show 'Fruit – God's results' in your sport?

Love:
I will show genuine concern for team-mates and ask them how they are doing and mean it.

Joy:
I will remind myself how God has given me the opportunity to compete.

Peace:
I will prepare harder for competitions and know that I have done all that I have done to be prepared with the talent God has given me.

Patience:
I will remember that team-mates may not respond the same way I do.

Kindness:
I will encourage team-mates and competitors.

Goodness:
I will assert a positive atmosphere in the locker-room.

Gentleness:
I will be gracious when I win and lose.

Self-control:
I will remember that God has given me great power and I will keep that power within the boundaries.

Reflection

Go back over the list of the fruits of the
Spirit and make your own practical list.

Prayer

God, please help me to endeavour to exhibit
a Christian behaviour in my sport.

*'By their fruit you will recognize them.   Do people
pick grapes from thorn-bushes or figs from thistles?'*
JESUS

Finish the Race

'Timothy, guard what has been entrusted to your care. Turn away from godless chatter and opposing ideas of what is falsely called knowledge, which some have professed and in so doing have wandered from the faith.'
1 TIMOTHY 6:20-21

A very worn Bible has a special home in my office on a shelf that I can reach easily. The book was a gift from a friend, an upperclassman and team-mate. He had two study-Bibles and knew I was broke and needed this Bible for a certain class. It was well used and well loved when I received it and I determined to use it as much as he obviously did. My friend wrote insightful comments in the margins and underlined several key verses that still give me valuable understanding of the scriptures! I love this Bible, though over the years it has lost it's cover and looks pretty beat. It is also a bittersweet story because my friend is far from walking with Christ at the moment. I can't say exactly what went wrong, but there has been a slow erosion in his soul and he has let his faith slide.

Paul wrote to his faithful young apprentice from a lonely prison cell. Most of Paul's friends had had enough, visiting folks in prison is a faithful task and many of Paul's friends seemed to disappear. Paul knew his ministry was finishing and a recurring theme to his young protégé with the sincere faith is: rekindle, don't be timid, don't be ashamed, guard the truth, be strong. Paul was concerned with Timothy's ministry and welfare and after seeing many friends come and go he wanted his 'beloved child' to finish strong. Timothy was warned to guard his heart. Any sports person that has succeeded knows the importance of staying focused, pushing oneself past the comfort zone and enduring. There will be times in your faith when you will seem to be the only one in the race, you may look around and ask where all your buddies have gone. That's okay – ask God to comfort and encourage you and enjoy the solitude.

Reflection

So guard what our Lord has entrusted to you
and grow strong and finish the race!

Prayer

Lord give me the endurance
to go the distance.

'I want you to become Old Oak Trees,
not weeds.'
ANDREW WINGFIELD DIGBY

Friendship

'One of them, the disciple whom Jesus loved, was reclining next to him…'
JOHN 13:23

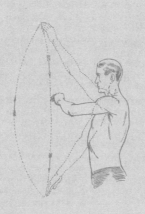

You learn a lot about yourself and your team-mates when you play on the road. Sometimes you are stuck on a flight next to a real bore and the time goes really slowly. Other times you can sit next to a good friend and the time seems to fly by. Friendship makes up one of the best parts of life. There is an intimacy with someone that makes you relax, someone you trust. When you are comfortable with someone you do not have to impress them. You do not mind them knowing you in every aspect of your life, the good, bad and the ugly. With friendship comes intimacy and new levels of interaction. Your friends are not perfect and neither are you. You may remember when a friend let you down and have forgotten when you let your friend down. But usually you remember the good times.

John was close to Christ, at dinner (the last supper) they 'reclined together'. Peter wanted to know a very important question so he elbowed John and said, 'you ask him'. We see a warm example of friendship as John leans back against Jesus and asks Him a question.

If Jesus, the perfect friend of sinners, were in this room right now in the flesh what level of friendship would you have with him? Would it be a formal relationship, stiff and superficial? Would you try to impress Him by name-dropping? Would you try to control the relationship, with a façade of self-righteousness? Would your own faults recoil you from Christ (The apostle Peter once said, 'get away from me Jesus') or could you have a relationship that was secure, warm and enjoyable. Jesus wants that depth of friendship, a companionship, which is a two-way thing. Christ wants to interact with you and you with Him. He wants to comfort and bless you and for you to bless Him. After you got past the excitement of meeting Jesus and got through every confession you needed to make with Christ, after you thought up every question about the world and eternity, would you have anything else to say? Have you built a friendship with Christ, could you enjoy His company?

Reflection
Do you know that Jesus likes you?

Prayer
Keep Satan's lies from me Lord and help me
to understand your friendship.

*'If I had to give a piece of advice to a young man
about a place to live, I think I should say,
'sacrifice almost everything to live where you can be
near your friends.'*
C.S. LEWIS

Guidance

*'Then they cast lots, and the lots fell to Matthias;
so he was added to the
eleven apostles.'*
ACTS 1: 26

So you are looking for God's will in your life? – what team to play for, what person to marry, which house to buy, which player to cut? Wouldn't it be nice to 'cast lots', like the apostles did to choose a new replacement for Judas! Wouldn't it be great to roll the dice and know that you were coming up on the right side of God's will every time!

So how come we do not see Christian leaders drawing 'lots' to make decisions in the Church, if it worked for Matthias? 'Casting lots' was a common procedure for seeking God's direction in the Old Testament. Could you see clergy throwing down stones and sticks with the decorating committee to decide the colour of their new carpets? The meetings would not be as long or as heated! Wouldn't it be funny to watch the 'Elders' of your church stop in the middle of a discussion to cast lots on whether to repair the old organ or buy a new one. Could you see a Christian coach throwing down sticks in a coaches meeting before choosing a new player? All these people want to make the right decisions for God! So why not cast lots?

Why not? Because Matthias was the last 'cast'! Never again will you find in the New Testament a follower of Christ using 'lots' to make their decisions. God has given us a gift much more powerful! The hallmark of the new age is the gift of the Holy Spirit! Never again are we to see a New Testament character use such a crude way of finding divine guidance, now we have the Holy Spirit our counsellor to steer us. Have you asked Christ to speak to you? It is usually very gentle but almost audible. Be still, ask God to clean you and be determined to try and stay clean. Next ask with determination and patience for guidance. Augustine had great advice for the Christian: Are you asking God for forgiveness, are you repenting and praying, are you hanging out with other believers and are you studying your scriptures? If you are doing all those things then don't worry, do what you want, God will show you His will.

Reflection

Delight yourself in the Lord always and He
will give you the desires of your heart.
Psalm 37:4

Prayer

Lord wrap my desires around your will!

*'So the Christian life is not a huge effort to do
good, but abdication of self and a prayer that God
will guide us through all the reefs.'*
GEORGE MACDONALD

Hope

'May the God of hope fill you with all joy and peace as you trust in Him, so that you may overflow with hope by the power of the Holy Spirit.'
ROMANS 15:13

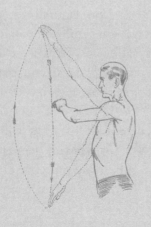

What are you putting your hope in? A recurring theme among professional sports people is trying to define themselves by possessions, appearance and performance. Many pros try to build their hope, self-esteem and function on things that do not last. Now granted, possessions, appearance and performance are nice to have and are not intrinsically wrong. In fact they are gifts from God to be used for God's pleasure and purpose. But when you put your intrinsic value in what you own, what you look like, (or your reputation) or how well you compete, you are setting yourself up for dissatisfaction and misery. Why? Because possessions, appearance and performance do not last! If **what** you value will not last, then **your** value will not last.

Hope and Joy are two qualities that the Christian can have regardless of external circumstances. Your car will rust, your looks will fade and your reflexes will slow down but God's value of you will never change. You will have bad days; you may have to playback your performance with annoyance. But when your hope is in God you will have an undercurrent of joy that will help you bounce back. Joy will run deeper than wins and losses. When you put your hope in God your joy will find its way out regardless of circumstances. Re-evaluate your self-worth by God's measure – it overflows!

Reflection

When your hope is based in universal truth
(For God so loved the world)
the by-product is joy.

Prayer

Praise to you Father for giving
this world hope.

*'Longevity has its place but I'm not concerned with
that now. I just want to do God's will. And he
has allowed me to go up to the mountain. And I've
looked over, and I've seen the promised land...Mine
eyes have seen the glory of the coming of the Lord.'*
MARTIN LUTHER KING JR.

Idols

What good will it be for a man if he gains the whole world yet forfeits his soul? Or what can a man give in exchange for his soul? For the son of man is going to come in his Father's glory with his angels, and then he will reward each person according to what he has done.'
MATTHEW 16: 26-27

I magine in your mind's eye: You feel a tap on your shoulder, you turn around and out of the blue is Jesus, and about one hundred million angels ready for battle. It feels strange that you have never seen Christ and yet you know without a doubt 'it is the Lord'. You know His presence and something inside you says you have been waiting for this moment all your life. Jesus says, 'Come on let's go home, now'. How would you respond? Yes, let's GO!! or 'But Jesus I have a big game tonight!' Or, 'I am hoping to be picked for a great honour I have worked for all my life!' 'Couldn't we wait just two days?'

A friend of mine asked me, 'If Jesus came back today would I be disappointed?'

I was amazed at how quickly things seemed to pop up in my head! I wanted to accomplish this or experience that before the 'Lord came back'. My friend advised me, 'Now you have found your idols, your God substitutes'. He went on to say: 'If anything is more important than our Lord; you have an idol, you have a problem'. We may think of idols as being ugly evil objects Satan uses in his bag of tricks. Actually most idols are good things in bad order; getting your priorities right is a lifelong balancing act. Idols can often be God-given talents. For example: 'I may want Jesus to come back soon, but first let me win that championship!' Championships are great! You may even be given a higher platform to share your faith in Christ after winning a title. However, if a championship is more important than being with Jesus you have an idol. My wife and I worked hard to retain sexual purity before we were married, (possibly the toughest spiritual challenge I have faced) and I was worried that Jesus was going to come back sometime between the wedding and the honeymoon (if you know what I mean!).

Beauty, sport, sex, money, children, reputation, power – these can be great God-given gifts; to be used for His glory and to enjoy. But in the wrong order they become idols and can have tragic consequences. So you have asked yourself 'If Jesus returned would I be disappointed?' A few things popped up in the computer screen of your mind. You will not be alone! Do not get down on yourself, but deal with it. Lay them at the foot of the cross. Remind yourself nothing is better than God. Put Him back on top and ask the Holy Spirit to help you keep God first!

Reflection
When goods become gods they're bads!

Prayer
Jesus you are my Master.

*'It must be put down as principal, that the use of
the gifts of God is not erroneous, when it is
directed to the same end for which the creator
Himself has created and appointed them for us;
since he has created them for our benefit,
not for our injury...'*
JOHN CALVIN

*'The dearest idol I have known,
What e're that idol be,
Help me to tear it from thy throne,
And worship only thee.'*
WILLIAM COWPER

I'm a Good Person

Wash me, and I will be whiter than snow. Let me hear joy and gladness; let the bones you have crushed rejoice. Hide your face from my sins and blot out all my iniquity. Create in me a pure heart.'
PSALM 51: 7-10

The church across the street from us is painted white. In fact a century or so years ago it was dubbed the 'White Church', and is quite famous. Sadly over the years the weather and pigeons had left their mark, the building was looking pretty weary. It was finally given a coat of nice fresh white paint. Now the church was once more looking clean and bright. The difference was remarkable and the change really brightened up the whole village. I was really impressed by the brilliance of the church and the freshness of the new paint job – until it snowed! The church looked pretty gloomy again against the backdrop of freshly fallen snow! In comparison to fresh snow the white church looked dingy.

The problem with a well-respected friend of mine is that his nature and disposition are really good! People like to be around him, he is funny, warm and witty. 'He probably thinks this section is about him'. He is charitable, caring and has no pretence. He is actually friendlier and more respected than many of the nice folks that go to his village church. He would say that he is a 'good person!' and I would have to agree. If our salvation were based on being good, I would suppose he would get a ticket with a gold star. Unfortunately in comparison to the purity of God he doesn't measure up!

We can all find someone that is by comparison less attractive, less smart, and less 'good' than ourselves. But in the pure light of God's magnificence we recognize that all have missed the mark and 'fall short of God's glory'. Take an honest look at yourself and you will see the need for forgiveness. You will also sense a deep gratitude for God's making us whiter than snow through Christ's sacrifice on the cross.

Reflection

When we realize that we don't measure up we are in a good position to ask God for help. When we understand we are dirty we can earnestly desire some cleaning.

Prayer

Father I realize the great need in my life for your forgiveness, make me pure, thank-you.

'I asked the guy next to me, 'How good are you from 1 to 10?—— that is, compared to Mother Teresa, not me!'
JERRY ROOT

Influence

Jesus said to his disciples: "Things that cause people to sin are bound to come, but woe to that person through whom they come. It would be better for him to be thrown into the sea with a millstone tied around his neck than for him to cause one of these little ones to sin. So watch yourselves".
Luke 17: 1-3

In our culture, sport is esteemed. Society esteems competitors. I remember watching my first American football game. I was in awe of these colossal titans! Their uniforms looked pristine, their power and speed was inspirational, their timing seemed super-human and the collisions were deliberate and explosive. To my young mind the atmosphere – shouts, cheers, the crack of colliding helmets, the combined smells of cut grass, athletic tape, deep-heat ointment, popcorn and cigar smoke – was intoxicating.

At half-time I observed both teams leave the field. The look of determination on their faces snapped me to attention as I paid tribute to their valiant efforts. This resolve was foreign to my experiences of playing football in the playgrounds and back-yards of Chicago. This instilled in me a healthy respect for an athlete's intensity; their strength-of-mind made me shudder. I felt rather silly licking my ice-cream cone while important men left the field to gather their forces for the up-coming battle. But one player stared right at me as he marched off with his team, he actually acknowledged me with a wry grin and a quick wink, and then he was gone. I was stunned, in the midst of such a crucial occasion this player set me aside for special acknowledgment. His team immediately became my team and for weeks I dreamed of playing his position, wearing his number, being him.

Sadly, I don't remember who he was, though his small gesture of kindness and the impression it made on me is still fondly burned into my memory. I was only five years old and he was only thirteen or fourteen! The teams playing that day were from the local High school's freshman squad. But when you are five and seeing your first game, thirteen year olds are giants!

If I knew you well enough I could find people that you have influenced. You do not have to be a pro to make an impact on others. Jesus understood that and gave a strict warning to 'watch ourselves' you are a role model, either a good one or a bad one.

Ask God to help you make a positive contribution in the lives of others, even in the lives of others you do not even know are watching you.

Reflection

What positive Christian role models have influenced you?

Prayer

Lord give me good role-models and noble virtues to dwell on.

'His infectious enthusiasm endeared him to the sporting public, and for the next four years he packed the terraces at every sports meeting he attended.'
D.P. THOMSON RECOUNTING ERIC LIDDELL

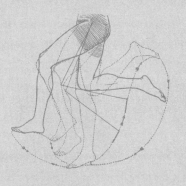

Life

*'We have this treasure in jars of clay to show that
this all-surpassing power is from God and not
from us.'*
2 Corinthians 4:7

I was standing at the sink of a grim damp mountain-side restroom shaking and feeling so sad as I watched the poor man's blood leave my hands and trickle down the sink. I had held the man in my hands earlier that morning and tried desperately to revive him; but he gasped and died. It seemed so disrespectful to simply let what had earlier that morning been part of a biological masterpiece now simply wash down a dirty drain.

Two cars behind him on an icy pass, I had watched him fight a losing battle on a patch of black ice. His breaks locked, he lost control and careered into a lorry (semi truck) coming from the other direction. The vehicle exploded before my eyes and I did what anyone would have done and tried to rescue him. It became a three-vehicle pile up and I ran to the closest vehicle. The first two drivers I met were both bloody and shaken, but in time would heal fast. The third was different. I turned to him with shock, foolishly I asked him if he was okay and got no response. Practising my rusty first aid I tried to keep his neck immobilized and his air passage clear, but he merely gasped involuntarily in my hands, then – dreary silence. I tried to tell him of Christ and prayed for him but no response, no pulse. His personal effects: magazine, glasses, coat were strewn around the road. I wanted to apologize to him as I realized

I had stepped on his pack lunch in the midst of the mayhem and ruined it. The finality hit me when I covered him with a blanket; I had to ask myself, 'who was I to make the statement that he was gone', but to not cover him would have been disrespectful. The accident was in a remote mountain pass and it took the police forty-five minutes to arrive. The road was blocked on both sides and the cars were backed up for miles. I stood dutifully like a sentry waiting to be relieved by the police. Men slowly got out of their cars and some came toward the wreck, in all probability out of a mixed sense of morbid curiosity (we all have it) and a desire to pay some type of respect for the dead man. As the sun slowly rose on that wintery Scottish pass I remember the grim faces of the onlookers who came to see the image of the man slumped in his vehicle with the blanket over him. The faces were all thinking the same thing, 'that could have been me and some day it will! What is this life all about?'

Human death strikes a chord with our own mortality. It reminds us that we will someday stop competing. As the man's blood went down the drain I remembered that life is not made up of calcium, blood and flesh, they are merely our vehicle. A clay pot to hold very special treasure. Life is our soul. We carry our life around in these clay jars. The jars crack and break; they are soon thrown away. Sometimes these clay pots are violently destroyed, but the content, the 'real deal' can live with God forever.

Today draw breath and draw near to God. Remember that this experiment of life on earth is a gift that is limited. Enjoy the small things like laughter and birds singing. Remember that through Christ, when that clay pot cracks, you will be released to your home in Heaven with your Father.

Reflection

You will live forever in Heaven or Hell.

Prayer

Father, some days I feel like I am going to live on earth forever. I know it is not true, help me to prepare well.

'Why, you do not even know what will happen tomorrow? What is your life? You are a mist that appears for a little while, then vanishes.'
JAMES 4:14

Motivation

'Therefore, I urge you, brothers, in view of God's mercy, to offer your bodies as living sacrifices, holy and pleasing to God — this is your spiritual act of worship.'
ROMANS 12:1

For the entertainment of his friends, an art student, in the 1930s pretended to be a Christian for the day. He went to Notre Dame Cathedral wearing drab clothes carrying a Bible and a crucifix. He walked humbly, in an almost mournful fashion. He did all the things he imagined other church goers did: he crossed himself with holy water, knelt, feigned prayer, bowed and lit candles. However, he was reluctant to go see the man. He did not want to go to confessional. Nevertheless, his two friends mockingly urged him on.

The young artist with false contrition mocked confession before the priest. Fortunately the priest was a wise and good man, he saw through the young pretender's lies. The priest said, 'For your sins I want you to go up to the front of the church and look at Christ suspended from the cross. I want you to say three times loud and clear, 'For what you have done for me, I do not give a damn!'" The artist was shocked, he thought to himself, 'Is this what they do in confessional?' He was reluctant to finish his charade, but something compelled him to obey the priest. So he marched up to the cross in the great Parisian Cathedral with a queer feeling in his gut. He saw Christ hanging on the cross, his face an intermingle of peace, sorrow and completion. He shocked himself at how irreverent he sounded as he performed his mock amends, 'Jesus for what you have…'. Quivering he again voiced the priest's instruction, 'Jesus, for what you have done for me… On his third declaration his whole body seemed to writhe in guilt as he felt the 'weight of Christ glory crush his arrogance and pride', he fell to the floor in tears. When he finally got off his knees he stood in full view of God's mercy as a new man in Christ.

In Romans 12 Paul shifts from his most excellent and sweeping explanation of God's 'grace' to the Christian's *response* to grace. He stops and urges his reader 'In view of God's mercy' live as a Christian. This is profound and one of the Christian hallmarks of truth. We respond to God's love and live for Him merely in response to what He has done for us – in view of God's mercy.

Reflection
Are my actions motivated by my
view of the cross?

Prayer
Lord you are so merciful to me,
help me to do better.

'We should study those verses for fifty years!'
MARK SCHMITT

Over-confidence

'In the Spring, at the time when kings go off to war, David sent Joab out with the king's men and the whole Israelite army ... but David remained in Jerusalem. One evening David got up from his bed and walked around on the roof of the palace. From the roof he saw a woman bathing. The woman was very beautiful ...'

2 SAMUEL 11:1 - 2

Savour victories with gratitude! Indelibly mark them in your mind for those long winter nights ahead of you. But guard your heart with diligence, keep your divine perspective and ask for protection.

If you are at all any good at sport you will end up in a dangerous spiritual position called victory. Learn to be dependent on God in times of success! In those hazardous periods when one is naturally inclined to draw on the chimera of personal strength, draw close to the Lord. Victory is wonderfully dangerous. Our inclination to be self-reliant is most pressing when we are on a roll. These are precarious times and we need to be cautious.

Evaluate your prayer life and ask yourself, 'Do I pray as much for God's guidance during a winning season as a losing season?'

When King David should have been leading his men in war, he stays home after enjoying a season of successive victories on the battlefield. The great hero of many victories falls into the seductive trap of success. Uncharacteristically the great warrior relaxes at home when he should have been, 'off to war'. In a season of triumph David lets his guard down and the consequences are adultery, murder and almost the downfall of his kingdom. Many leaders bow their knee in humility during personal tragedy. Wise leaders bow to the King of kings in those seasons of victory. Enjoy those wins – they are a gift from God, but stay on your knees!

Reflection

Sure, most people pray during a crisis, but will I stay close to God during a winning season?

Prayer

Father teach me to be close to you in the good times.

'Arrogance is God's gift to shallow people.'
DENNIS WAITLEY

Patience

*Be still before the Lord and wait patiently for him;
do not fret when men succeed in their ways, when
they carry out their wicked schemes.'*
PSALM 37:7

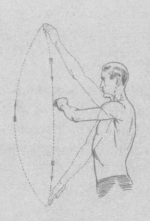

atience is a most aggressive, pro-active virtue. Patience is an art for warriors. There is no better thing we can do than to wait upon the Lord. Waiting on God puts your trust into God's lap and there is no other place secure for yourself. Being still before God in communion with the creator of the Universe helps give clarity and focus to your will. God's son taught all who follow him to call God 'Abba', 'Dear Father'. There is a world of clutter vying for your thoughts, we are obsessed with the chain of events; and yet it is our supernatural status, which affects our world.

'Do not fret' – so what is the absence of fretting? Having a deep confidence that God (Your Daddy) is working on your side for your supreme good. A non-fretter will understand that God works all things out for His good. You will experience pain, loss, death and embarrassment, but God will work it all out. When your satisfaction comes from knowing God and enjoying him for eternity, your comfort rests in Him.

The death rate in Scotland is still 100 per cent, all the fretting in the world will not change it! During a certain personal stressful period in my life (after a sporting knee injury) my dear friend told me, 'Worry is an alarm in your head to remind you to pray'. My retort,

'If I listen to your advice I will pray without ceasing'. So, I prayed and prayed and prayed. It was not always pleasant and not always comforting. Sometimes my prayers were rich and sometimes waiting on God was merely duty. No exterior supernatural miracles occurred but I still, fifteen years later, feel the blessings from those prayers. Patience is an art form for tough people.

Reflection

Most people I know in the world of sport
are pro-active! They know how to make
things happen! Be a pro-active pray-er
besides a pro-active player.
Pray hard – life is short!

Prayer

Lord give me the confidence in the season
of waiting, to know you are with me, to
trust you have the best for me.

'A man's wisdom gives him patience'
PROVERBS 19:11

Perseverance

'Therefore since we are surrounded by such a great cloud of witnesses, let us throw off everything that hinders and the sin that so easily entangles, and let us run with perseverance the race marked out for us. Let us fix our eyes on Jesus, the author and perfecter of our faith, who for the joy set before him endured the cross, scorning its shame, and sat down at the right hand of the throne of God.'
HEBREWS 12:1-2

How could you have a sports devotional and not draw on Hebrews chapter twelve. The imagery puts you in the tunnel of a packed stadium. You are introduced to a cheering crowd as you make your entrance onto the field. Instead of fans cheering for you, the cheers are coming from former greats of the game. The role has been reversed! Instead of you cheering for your old heroes, your heroes are cheering for you. Instead of having a 'home-field advantage' you have one better, a 'home of heroes', advantage. If you could not be motivated to do your utmost and play your heart out in front of the greatest of the game, you will never be motivated.

The scriptures urge us to rid ourselves of any burden that will slow us down, or trip us up. In front of a great crowd, we would look ridiculous trying to play American football whilst carrying a ball and chain. Imagine playing soccer in a wet muddy suit, or playing tennis carrying a backpack full of horse manure. You want to play at your best and you recognize that means playing unhindered. Sports manufacturers invest millions to create sportswear that doesn't encumber the performer.

The writer of Hebrews must have seen people who enter into the race of life with great determination only to be dragged down and tripped up by sin. We are given very clear instruction; plainly, we are to fix our eyes on Christ. We know the victory Christ won for us and the great race He ran, so follow Him. The best way to teach a concept is to model it. See Christ's endurance, determination, focus, patience and strong- mindedness. Hear the crowd of Christ's followers cheering you on as you run your race. Jesus is our model. All the bad things that drag us down, that once seemed so important in life will now seem hideously encumbering and suffocating. You will want to jettison the immaterial and the decaying baggage when your eyes are fixed on Jesus. So lighten your load, feel your pace quicken and hear those old heroes cheering you on!

Reflection
Let go, let God!

Prayer
What ever is tripping me up and choking me out, Lord help me to rid myself of it; keep me focused on you.

'Who can't fight good when the crowd is behind you.'
MUHAMMAD ALI

Playing by the Rules

'One day after Moses had grown up, he went out to where His own people were and watched them at their hard labour. He saw an Egyptian beating a Hebrew, glancing this way and that and seeing no one, he killed the Egyptian and hid him in the sand.'
EXODUS 2:11–12

It is not uncommon for pro-active people to act out of impulse, almost unconsciously they try and force God's hand. With spiritual maturity we understand that He will not be manipulated. When Moses was young he tried to take his destiny in his own hands. Little is known about Moses' childhood. Pharaoh's daughter raised him as royalty after Moses was rescued from her father's sanction that all first-born Jewish boys must die. It is reasonable to assume Moses was trained as a prince, his privileged upbringing would have given him many skills that he would later use; including writing, tactical warfare and chariot combat. Moses knew he was a Hebrew and for many years he saw his people subjugated. Moses must have burned inside, craving to see justice done in the lives of the Hebrew slaves. Coming upon an Egyptian soldier beating a defenceless Hebrew slave, Moses' pent-up hatred surfaces; he intervenes and murders the Egyptian.

We may rightly burn with indignation when exposed to injustice, but we need to stay within God's rules and fight in God's ways. Working outside of God's borders even when the reasons are good, ends up fruitless and destructive. If you perceive God to be incapable of acting unless you intervene in your own destructive ways, you have a poor understanding of God's power. He is the almighty and has set universal laws of justice. When we overstep those limits even with fine intentions (though those intentions are usually a smokescreen for internal evil desires) we damage God's cause and hurt others and ourselves. God's principals for eternity prevail. Have patience and ask God to give you shrewd insight in the fight against injustice for Him. Then respond with zeal knowing you are acting as God's envoy in God's way.

James and John – two of Jesus' top guys (apostles) were angered after Jesus was not welcomed in a certain Samaritan village. Their response was to ask Jesus for permission to 'call down fire from Heaven' and destroy the place! Jesus told them off and went to another village. At least James and John asked for permission before they tried to do something stupid!

Reflection

Understand God's power, He wants you to fight for Him, on His team, but in His ways.

Prayer

Father forgive me when I have done my own selfish thing, in your name.

'Human nature is to go to the bathroom in your pants. That, after all is the way each of us started out; doing what came naturally, letting go whenever we felt like it.'
M. SCOTT PECK

Power Manifested

'Instead, speaking the truth in love, we will in all things grow up into him who is the Head, that is, Christ.'
EPHESIANS 4:15

An antidote only works if it has been accessed personally. Penicillin only works when it is absorbed into the blood stream, it is rather useless sitting on a shelf, it only saved the lives of people who took it. God sent His Son to have victory over sin, and Jesus won the war. But His Son can only work His saving power through the individuals who access Him. Wouldn't it be evil if penicillin was not given to others – there are many countries that do not have access to life-saving drugs. Could you watch others die and not tell them that all they needed to fight the infection was penicillin. We have been given the antidote for sin in the form of Christ and when we access the Saviour, He gives us access to God.

The key to Christian growth is not just trying to be like Jesus, but allowing Jesus to spread His strength through the core of your being. The more He spreads through you, the more you respond like Him. Manifestation is an important word to understand. It is not just trying to emulate Jesus, which would be like having a disease and pretending to be healthy, without using the antidote. Instead, you have been given a power inside you that needs to be drawn on, and that power will affect your outward being. The antidote (faith in Christ) brings spiritual health, a spiritual restoration.

This spiritual health usually grows fast in some areas of our life and slowly in others. You will have some spiritual penchants that will take off with little prompting; other areas of your life will need more work. Some people only get spiritually healthy when they are challenged, usually by physical or mental stress. Our physical muscles, when given proper exercise, react to stimulus quickly and powerfully. An exercised muscle will be stronger and suppler. Disuse of muscles will bring on atrophy. Our spiritual muscles are similar. The more they are challenged, the more we allow Christ to be 'manifest' in us, the more we grow.

Reflection

Just as your physical body needs to be pushed to improve, so your soul needs to be pushed to improve. When you come up to that spiritual hurdle you want to be ready.

Prayer

Lord, I want to be prepared for the battle. Make me strong.

'May the supreme comforter, the Spirit of truth, possess your heart and comfort you.'
JORDAN OF SAXONY

'We don't get strong by talking about His power – we get strong by plugging into His power.'
JACK VANDIVER

Praise

'The heavens declare the glory of God, the skies proclaim the work of His hands.'
PSALM 19:1

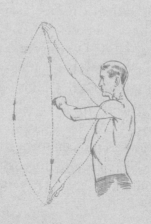

Look up at the sky and let God speak to you. God is on a massive public-relations campaign with His creation. It is a great confirmation to faith just looking at nature. God communicates in various ways; through the Holy Spirit, scripture, prayer, Christian friends and nature. Perceiving the Father, Son and Holy Spirit were involved together in creating this wonderful universe, with its material and spiritual matter, is core to a healthy Christian life.

An eminent philosopher said his faith crumbled when he could get no answer to the question: 'If God made the world, who made God?' God would not be who He is, if someone created Him. But let us take that presupposition, 'who made God' and try to answer it. Who made God? A super-God made God. Okay who made the super-God? A super-super-God made the super-God. Oh, well who made the super-super-God? A more, super-super-God made the super-super-God. Do you see the futility in the question? God is God. If he were 'made' He would not be God. God is self-existent; all other forms are created and have a beginning.

This is a short thought today (for you guys that don't like to read). Stop right now and look up into the sky. Try to imagine the millions of galaxies, planets and stars. The universe is God's playground. Let's 'Give it up for God.'

Reflection

There is something inside me that was designed to praise my Creator.

Prayer

Forgive me when my praise is directed poorly. Here and now please examine my heart, and accept my praise of you: Dear Lord and Saviour.

'I'm afraid that God is speaking but that no-one's listening.'
DANA SCULLY, THE X-FILES

Prayer
'Dear Father'

*'One day Jesus was praying in a certain place.
When He finished, one of His disciples said to
Him, 'Lord, teach us to pray, just as John taught
his disciples.' He said to them, "When you pray,
say: Father, hallowed be your name".'*
LUKE 11:1-2

Have you ever sat in a locker room whilst being chewed out by a coach or manager? Sometimes you hear the coach make adjustments and improve your personal and team's performance. Sometimes, especially if the coach only knows how to scream, all you hear is a dull drone; if you do not respect him, you learn to tune him out. Look around and watch your team — are they listening intently or are they staring at the floor with glazed eyes?

Jesus was a master teacher but He knew that over the centuries, His teachings might become trivialized. We have to ask God to keep us alert and careful. We must fight hard to keep His instructions fresh. Jesus warned His disciples that when you pray, don't say things over and over and not really mean them. Whenever we do pray the same prayer over and over it loses its punch, unless you concentrate on the meaning and align your body, spirit and mind with your prayer and His instruction. Jesus' teachings are not trite religious sentiment but rather a spiritual force that cuts to the heart of our life, like a 'double-edged sword'. One of the most badly abused teachings is when Jesus taught us to pray. He warned us in the gospel of Matthew not to 'babble', trying to impress God with 'many words'. Often the 'Lord's Prayer' is said out of superstition, (a lucky charm before a match) losing its meaning, purpose and power.

In our verse today we see Jesus' top-guys asking their master to teach them to pray. They have watched Him pray many times and watching others pray sincerely is contagious. Jesus' first word of his model prayer must have been shocking to the religious establishment of the time. They were taught to come to God in great fear and respect, so much so that they were rarely to even use God's name. Now Jesus says, 'Father'. Many have said that prayer from rote memory, but if you heard that prayer through the ears of a first century Jew it must have sounded so radical. Jesus was teaching His followers to approach and talk to the almighty God in the same way a child would approach a good dad. Jesus uses 'Abba' – an Aramaic word that would express the softer form of Father, more like Daddy. Jesus teaches that as believers we can intimately come to God the same way my daughter wakes from a scary dream and yells for Daddy, or my young son runs up to me with a book and requests me to read to him, 'please Daddy, read me a story'. The creator of the universe desires an intimate relationship with you through Christ and watches your life and performance with as much pride as any parent .

Reflection

Can you follow Jesus' advice and come to
the King of the Universe as a humble son or
daughter and address Him as
Dear Father (Daddy).

Prayer

Our Father in Heaven, help me to
understand your parenthood.

'You are all sons of God through faith in Christ.'
GALATIANS 3:26

Prayer
Bother the Big Man

'According to His eternal purpose which He accomplished in Christ Jesus our Lord. In Him and through faith in Him we may approach God with freedom and confidence...For this reason I kneel before the Father, from whom His whole family in heaven and earth derives its name.'
EPHESIANS 3:11-15

A tough old rugby player asked me to officiate at his marriage; I do not think he could find any other minister to do it! I agreed though being in sports ministry I do very few weddings and funerals. At the end of my conversation with him I said, 'God Bless you'! He declared in a tone of self-assurance, 'Oh no. You do not bother the big man, not unless you have a real tough problem!' I said, 'Where did you get that twaddle? You do not know much about this God who wants to have an intimate relationship with you. Have you heard that His Son taught us to call God 'Father' and a good Father cares about every aspect of His child's life?' I rather suspect the crusty old rugby player did not want to 'bother the Big Man' because God was on the sidelines of his life. The man was far from God and did not want God to sort him out.

God gives us a very special and intimate access to Him through his Son Jesus Christ. Intimacy means time together – prayer.

I remember sitting in a buddy's pick-up truck when he quickly explained to me a very helpful pattern for prayer; the acronym ACTS: **A**doration, **C**onfession, **T**hanksgiving and **S**upply. This was useful and gave me a balanced perspective for praying. I want to add another letter L, which stands for **L**istening. Maybe this will be a good pattern for you, maybe it won't. Not everybody is a fast pitch bowler. Not everybody can throw the hammer; if it does not work for you find something that does.

  Adoration
  Confession
  Thanksgiving
  Supply
  Listen

The key is knowing we can come to the Father anytime we want in 'freedom and confidence'.

Reflection
Am I afraid of approaching God because
there are issues in my life I would rather not
deal with? So then – who wins if I stay
away from God?

Prayer
Father help me to pray.

*'The Lord is near to all who call on him, to all
who call on him in truth. He fulfils the desires of
all who fear him; he hears their cry
and saves them.'*
PSALM 145:18

Prayer
Adoration

*'I will exalt you, my God the King; I will praise
your name for ever and ever. Everyday I will
praise you and extol your name for ever and ever.'*
PSALM 145: 1-2

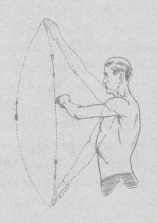

We were created to praise, there is something inside us that is fulfilled by adoration; if you do not believe me watch normal people transform into screaming fans at their favourite sporting event (interestingly, you are a fan at a sporting event but if you get excited about God you are labelled a 'fanatic'). We love to cheer for our favourite team; we give praise and esteem to a fine wine and watch some guys get misty-eyed as they wax eloquently over the qualities of a new car. So how much more should we give due praise to the Creator of the universe! He is worthy. Giving praise to God may be new to you, it can feel awkward. Satan will whisper in your ear that you are not worthy to give God praise! That is a magnificently subtle lie, for you are His children and He loves you to draw near to Him.

Think of some of the many attributes of God: He is compassionate, all-powerful, saving, everywhere, intimate, wrathful, jealous... Remember God is not an egotist, but He knows that when his children praise Him it brings them into clarity, focus and spiritual health with their Heavenly Father. It is the best. And at times it is hard work.

I remember my coach telling me that when his prayers were dry he would go to an expert on prayer – He went to David in the Psalms. Let me encourage you to do the same. Adore your God and praise him with your heart. Feel yourself coming into the presence of the King of kings with words of adoration on your lips. When you praise God – Father, Son and Holy Spirit – you are in the best position to pray. You have put yourself in the right posture and set your Lord as top precedence in your life. Let your praise to the Almighty God release you to a special time of prayer with God.

When you watch a game in a professional stadium, or even a tug of war match in your local village, you realize that people love to cheer and shout. We were made for worshipping. Our only problem is directing our worship to the right source. If you have ever been in a sprint race you know what it is like to let the starter's gun release you to fly down the track. Let praise for our Creator focus and release you to a deeper sense of prayer. Praising God gives us better perspective, intimacy and priority.

Reflection

As you give praise to God, you will align your will with God's as your relationship with Him falls into place.

Prayer

Psalm 147: 1 'Praise the Lord. How good it is to sing praises to our God, how pleasant and fitting to praise him.'

'We are drifting towards a religion which consciously or unconsciously keeps its eye on humanity rather than on Deity – which lays all the stress on service, and hardly any of the stress on awe.'
EVELYN UNDERHILL

Prayer
Confession

'If we confess our sins, he is faithful and just and will forgive us our sins and purify us from all unrighteousness.'
1 JOHN 1:9

onfession is the first step in turning to forgiveness. If we break a rule and deny it, how can we be forgiven? If you deny you have a wound how will you ever heal it? If you ignore your sin it will fester and grow worse. Owning up to wrongs is a noble act of humility. God knows that humility is a great source of spiritual health, which restores your relationship to God and others. Having children has given me great lessons in confession. Children make mistakes all day long, kids will never move ahead by denying their wrongs unless they admit it when they make them, and not pretend they have not done wrong. I never tire of hearing earnest confession from them. This has helped me realize that God will not tire of me coming to my Heavenly Father with a sincere spirit of confession. The benefit of purity before God is wonderful; it is a battle we will fight our whole life.

At university I was close to three ministers. Two of them seemed to have an appearance of perfection; I put them on a pedestal. Looking back, those first two ministers never discouraged my reverence of them, they seemed like pillars of perfection. But the first two did not have the impact on me that the third minister had. I still remember him teary-eyed in his pulpit confessing some sin he had recently committed. His confession must have jarred every man in his church because they were common to us all. But this minister took sin seriously and as pastor of a big church he felt the responsibility of his position. I can relate to the third minister because I am not perfect and needed to watch a man who was brave enough to admit that he was not perfect and needed Christ to forgive him. Incidentally, the first two ministers are out of the ministry because they both had committed adultery. The third has had an international ministry serving His Lord and Saviour.

Confess your sin and keep short accounts with God. Christ shed His blood so we can shed our muck.

Reflection

How good and freeing it is to be pure before the Lord. Confess your sins.

Prayer

Have mercy on me O God, according to your unfailing love; according to your great compassion blot out my transgressions. Wash away all my iniquity and cleanse me from my sin.

Psalm 51:1-2

'As far as the east is from the west, so far has he removed our transgressions from us.'

PSALM 103: 12

Prayer
Thanksgiving

'Be joyful always; pray continually; give thanks in all circumstances, for this is God's will for you in Christ Jesus.'
1 THESSALONIANS 5:16-17

If I knew you well I could find many things that you could give genuine thanks to God for! Thanksgiving acknowledges the source of the gift. Whether it is physical, spiritual, mental or social, God has lavished you with gifts which deserve your appreciation. Expressing our gratitude to God keeps the focus and due praise on our Lord and helps us keep our relationship with Him in proper perspective. We are reminded to give thanks in all circumstances.

Know that one of God's attributes is transcendence; He is perpetually shaping and permeating the world for His glory. God understands the big picture and will work out all things for His glory. This may not seem helpful to you in a real crisis. Maybe you have someone close to you that has died, perhaps you have been cut from a team that you have longed to play for. There is no easy answer for you right now. No easy words that will take that pain away. Remember you were never promised that in this world you would not have pain or suffering.

I am asking God to comfort you right now through the pain. You may say 'what a joke, you do not know my situation.' You are right, I do not. In fact, even if I knew you personally I probably would not completely understand all you are going through. But our Lord knows you so intimately and he knows when you are reading this, so I again pray that the Father would comfort you, help you to see, know His love and give you a grateful heart.

Reflection

You have gifts and abilities that were given to you by God. During the down times in your life they may not as easily be seen by yourself. Those times are exactly the times to ask God to give you a grateful heart.

Prayer

Thank you for_____. It is a special talent or gift I had never thought of before.

Be joyful always; pray continually; give thanks in all circumstances, for this is God's will for you in Christ Jesus.'
1 THESSALONIANS 5:16-18

Prayer
Supply

*'Delight yourself in the Lord and He will give you
the desires of your heart.'*
PSALM 37:4

Notice that supply is at the end of this pattern for prayer. Often we gravitate to the 'gimme-this-gimme-that' mode of prayer. Jesus is not a 'genie in a bottle' and much of what we ask for is not what we need. I found this poem helpful.

I asked God for strength that I might achieve.
I was made weak that I might learn humbly to obey.

I asked God for health that I might do greater things. I was given infirmity that I might do better things.

I asked for riches that I might be happy. I was given poverty that I might be wise.

I asked for power that I might have the praise of men. I was given weakness that I might feel the need of God.

I asked for all things that I might enjoy life. I was given life that I might enjoy all things.

I got nothing that I asked for – but everything I had hoped for...
Almost despite myself my unspoken prayers were answered.
I am among all men most richly blessed.

(Unknown Confederate Soldier of the American Civil War.)

After you have adored God, confessed your sin (acknowledging Jesus as your Lord and Saviour who has supreme authority to forgive sin), thanked God for all He has done for the world and you personally; you will be in a healthy attitude to ask God for whatever you want. When you delight in the Lord and want His desires for your own, your desires fall better into place. God's desires become your desires. When I look through Jesus' eyes my selfish desires fade a bit more and my wants are more for what God wants. Christ modelled a prayer for us as He was in deep suffering; agonizing over prayer, He pronounced to His Father 'not my will but yours be done'.

God wants to equip you, but to equip you for His purposes. If God answered all the prayers you prayed this week, how many people would become Christians? No, I did not say how many goals you would score, but how many of your team-mates would become Christians? Bring your friends before the throne of your Heavenly Father. Ask God to work in their lives and yours.

Ask God to equip you to reach your family, your team-mates and the world for Christ. You will have specific material needs: bring them before Him. Remember God will never tire of your prayers and your prayers will mature the more time you spend with Him.

Reflection

The more you open your soul to God, the more you allow him to cultivate and nourish your inner self.

Prayer

Father give me your desires.

'The noble inclination whereby man thirsteth after riches and dominion is his highest virtue, when rightly guided; and carries him as in a triumphant chariot, to his sovereign happiness. Men are made miserable only by abusing it. Taking a false way to satisfy it, they pursue the wind.'

THOMAS TRAHERNE

Prayer
Listen

'Then a great and powerful wind tore the mountains apart and shattered the rocks before the Lord, but the Lord was not in the wind. After the wind there was an earthquake, but the Lord was not in the earthquake. After the earthquake came a fire, but the Lord was not in the fire. After the fire came a gentle whisper. When Elijah heard it, he pulled on his cloak over his face and went out and stood at the mouth of the cave.'
1 KINGS 19: 11-13

Sometimes God speaks in big things, but often we have to be still and wait on Him.

It is easier to tell God what you want than to hear what God wants for you. Sometimes I do not want to hear God, because He is notorious for telling His followers to do seemingly crazy things: like apologizing to a friend or family member, loving someone different from me, or encouraging me to give away a bit more money and time. God is like a coach; a good coach makes his players do what they don't want to do (like train hard), so they will achieve what they want to achieve (win). God may tell you to do something that you do not want to do (like tell the truth), so you become what you want to become (respected).

It is not always hard to hear what God wants to say to you, allow Him to lavish His love on you, be still and wait for Him. If you hear Him speak, write it down and test it against scripture. Some people have given me 'words from God' that have simply been manufactured in their imagination. Sometimes God speaks through a powerful conviction that emerges in our hearts; you know that acting on that conviction is acting on God's wish. He is often quiet – just enjoy His presence and be still.

Remembering the attributes of God whilst in His presence can be helpful.

Psalm 48:9 'We meditate on your unfailing love.' He is a King that deserves all awe and respect; He is all-powerful, everywhere, self-existent and creative. God is perfect love and desires His creation to draw near to Him and honour Him. God is quick to forgive and wants to lavish His love on you.

Psalm 37:7 'Be still before the Lord and wait patiently for Him'.

Reflection

How do I treat God – as a genie, 'grant me
three wishes' or like Samuel who said:
'Speak Lord for your servant is listening.'

Prayer

Speak Lord for you servant is listening.

*'They all serve to remind us of what we are and
who God is – that we may get sick of the sight of
ourselves and turn to Him: and in the end, we will
find Him in ourselves, in our own purified natures
which have become the mirror of His tremendous
goodness and of his endless love...'*
THOMAS MERTON

Prayer
Protection

*'Lead me not into temptation
and deliver me from evil.'*
MATTHEW 6:13

One final point I want to stress on prayer. There is a curious and extremely important phrase for sports people at the end of the Lord's prayer: *Matthew 6:13 'lead me not into temptation and deliver me from evil.'*

Jesus gave us a pattern for prayer that pleads for protection. There are some battles we should not be fighting. Maybe we will fight these spiritual battles when we are stronger or more mature Christians. Maybe there are some things we should never fight! Remember there is a real, active personal power in opposition to God, sometimes we should just ask God to get us out of there, fast, 'deliver me from evil'! We need to understand that we are weak and need God's huge fortress – humbly asking God for His protection is wise. A cavalier attitude to temptation has brought down many a great Christian leader.

Self-sufficiency is a dangerous, unbiblical theme that permeates the world of sport. Nobody likes an egotist, but in sport there is a subtle influence that implies, 'you need to rely on yourself'. 'Have faith in yourself', is a cherished slogan among coaches. Self-sufficiency runs counter to Christianity. People involved in sport as well as other areas of human excellence are trained to believe that if we really want something badly enough and work hard enough for it we can achieve it.

Many good Christian coaches and competitors perpetuate bad theology by blending messages of self-centred human performance and biblically-based Christ-centred human performance. These influences propagate an attitude of, 'since God is on my side I can take on anything!' 'I am invincible!' Do not use this as an excuse to turn off your coach. Rather stay close to the scriptures and test philosophies of life by God's Word. When you are not sure, find someone who can help. Jesus taught us to rely on Him. Ask for his protection.

Reflection

Meditate on the protection you have in
Christ when you ask for it.

Prayer

My prayer is not that you take them out of
the world but that you protect them from
the evil one.

John 17:15

*'But let all who take refuge in you be glad; let them
ever sing for joy. Spread your protection over them.'*
PSALM 5:11

Preparation

*'Peter saw the opportunity
and addressed the crowd!'*
ACTS 3:12

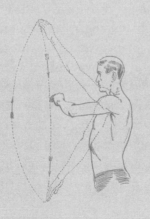

So Peter saw an opportunity to proclaim His master. He saw the opening and went for it. Have you been trained to share your faith, in real words, to tell others what the saviour of the universe has done for you and what Jesus can do for your friend? Consider this: we are trained in so many ways, we are taught to read, to drive, we are coached in our various sports but when it comes to communicating such crucial information to others, we seem to leave it to chance.

I remember the first time I bench pressed The weight was pretty light and the bar was very unstable as I tried to shove it off my chest, I had to face the facts – I was a weakling! But through time and coaching, my muscles and form developed, I got in the weight room and worked hard. As I matured physically, the weight training improved. Several years later I started lifting with a friend who has his PhD in Kinesiology. I thought I knew something about weight training. After about two months of serious soreness and a lot of coaching, my competence improved again. Getting some coaching and encouragement helps.

I remember sharing my faith for the first time; I was terrified, big time! My coach (both spiritual and football coach) challenged me to tell a young teenage boy about Christ. It was a pretty sorry effort and I probably confused the poor guy more than I helped him. But my coach was there and helped both of us through the 'Good News'. I was terrible, but at least it was a start. God does not expect you to start off as a spiritual giant! But He does want you to get in there and try. Look for the opportunities to share your faith with friends, colleagues and classmates. Are you prepared to clearly communicate the Gospel of Jesus Christ? Get some coaching, and then start coaching others to proclaim Christ clearly and genuinely. It will last a lot longer than big biceps!

Reflection

Peter's friends once prayed that he would be miraculously released from jail. When he was, they weren't prepared to receive him. We ask God for our friends to come to Christ – when they are willing, are we prepared to show them the way?

Prayer

Father, prepare me to boldly and clearly give good answers when those tough questions come along.

'Every man is guilty of all the good he did not do.'
VOLTAIRE

'Three things come not back: the spoken word, the spent arrow and the lost opportunity.'
PROVERB

Purity

*'Drink water from your own cistern, running water
from your own well... May your fountain be
blessed, and may you rejoice in the wife of your
youth... may her breasts satisfy you always, may you
always be captivated by her love.'*
PROVERBS 5:15-19

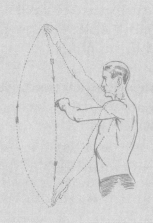

Why don't you swallow a cup of table salt and wash it down with a gallon of sea water. That is what you are doing if you fool around with sex outside of marriage. You are putting something into your system that will only hurt you, then trying to satisfy it with more of the same poison. It is no wonder Mick Jagger can't get any satisfaction! Sin is unsatisfying and the sin of lust is subtle, it will frustrate and poison you and, like a nicotine addiction, force you to desire the problem not the solution. What you do with your body will affect your spirit.

Sexuality is a precious gift and virginity should be given away, not taken. Sexual intercourse is an endowment of oneness with a spouse. Sex is a commitment of you, completely and joyfully, giving pleasure and something of unique spiritual unity to a spouse. Scripture's instructions are that in marriage, couples are to fulfil each other sexually. Today's Bible verse says that a wise person will be satisfied (actually intoxicated) by their spouse's love.

God's message is clear that inside marriage sexuality is a wonderful exploration of unity. Marriage and sexuality is a system created by God. Obedience to that system, staying inside the boundaries of His plan, gives fulfilment and purpose. But sexuality is also a powerful and dangerous force that, when explored outside of God's boundaries, has injured and broken many people. Western culture has all but given up on 'God's system' of sexual purity and the destructive effects are all around us. The message you hear about sexual purity will be contradicted cunningly, and unashamedly in the media several times a day. It may be your toughest spiritual battle. Sexuality, the chemistry of the opposite and sometimes the same sex, is so remarkably strong (sex sells almost everything). As a fourteen year old what scared me most about committing myself to Christ was committing to sexual purity. The draw to sex is amazing and I was almost willing to forfeit my soul. Fortunately, Christ is more compelling and sport taught me something of discipline and delayed gratification. I also learned after making many mistakes that Satan would lie to me and whisper to my conscious, 'God will have nothing to do with you – you are unworthy to go back to Him!' It is a horrid lie and if you have to pick yourself off the floor one hundred times every day, keep returning to Christ with an attitude of forgiveness, He will be there for you over and over. Slowly, your habits will change, you will grow sick of your sin and you will desire God's desires most of all. May you also enjoy the benefits, the sweet intoxication, of His system.

Reflection

This may be your toughest battle. Fight hard and when you are knocked down, get up fast. Satan will lie to you and say you do not deserve to go before God in confession. Don't listen, run to the Lord and ask for His forgiveness and strength.

Prayer

May your unfailing love be my comfort...
Psalm 119:76

'The orgasm has replaced the Cross as the focus of longing and the image of fulfilment.'
MALCOLM MUGGERIDGE

Purity

If you keep yourself pure, you will be a utensil God can use for his purpose. Your life will be clean, and you will be ready for the Master to use you for every good work.'
2 TIMOTHY 2:21

Competition gives a sense of urgency. There is nothing like a competitive match to help focus your attention. While competing, you are robustly analysing, defining and honing your mutual and personal strengths. Disciplining yourself to train hard in the off-season can be more difficult. The competition seems far away. In the off-season, you need a strong devotion to your sport; you need to value your goals. When you have a plan for improving your performance, your off-season training regime will be meaningful. If the payout at the end is worth it, you can train hard even if your goals seem far into the future.

Therefore, spiritual discipline should (I wrote 'should') be easy! To stand before the Father and hear, *'Well done good and faithful servant'* at the end of your life, must be the ultimate award. Can you envisage a better incentive? If you look into the lenses of 'infinity' can you find a better trophy, a higher honour or more prestigious medal than God's approval? What is going to last in your life?

When we were called by Christ, we were put into battle. Heaven may seem like a long way off but we really don't have a spiritual off-season. Paul encourages us to keep pure, so we can be used by God! God wants to use you and he can maximize your effort by your purity and devotion to him. This is our sense of urgency. Our purpose as followers of Christ is God's purpose. This sharpens us and gives us internal direction. Then, 'you will be ready for the Master to do good work.' That day will come when every knee will bow before Him. Don't waste your time – go for gold! Go, for the: 'Well done good and faithful servant!'

Reflection

In team sports it is a great feeling to be a valued member and make a significant impact in a game. The same is true on God's team, you are valued as a 'pure utensil' used by God for His purposes.

Prayer

Father, make me an impact player for you.

'Preach the gospel at all times,
when necessary use words.'
St. Francis of Assisi

Risk

*'His master replied, "Well done good and faithful
servant! You have been faithful with a few things;
I will put you in charge of many things. Come and
share your master's happiness."'*
MATTHEW 25:21

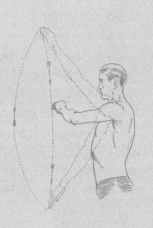

One of my favourite lines in the movie *Chariots of Fire*, comes after Harold Abrahams, a brilliant sprinter, loses the first race of his career. In a moment of weakness, he decides to quit running and looking at his girl friend says, 'If I cannot win, I will not race!' Her response is shrewd, 'If you do not race, you cannot win!' Sport is a microcosm of life. In a two-hour competition, you may experience a lifetime's emotion. You win, lose, succeed, and fail. You observe and incur frustration, agony, stress, joy, satisfaction, achievement, euphoria and letdown. If you do not compete, you may never feel the pain of losing but you will never know the joy of winning. In competition, you put yourself on the line – you take risks.

Christians should be the greatest risk takers.

Tape a one hundred pound note to the end of an eight-inch wide, twelve-foot long steel beam placed on the ground. Explain to a friend, if they walk across the beam, and pick up the money they may keep it. No problem! However, change the conditions by securing the beam out of the top window of the Sears Tower in Chicago over one thousand feet in the sky. The challenge of picking up the money becomes harder. My father helped build the Sears Tower. Working with him one summer I was amazed at how effortlessly he could walk those beams. He would say, 'it's just the same as walking across the garden, except if you fall in your garden you push down daisies, if you fall off a building you push up daisies!'

Jesus taught his disciples to take risks. To use the gifts and abilities God had given them for his glory. The Bible does not ever say that a life in Christ will be easy, you may be called to live and serve in another country, you may have to face jeers from team-mates, you may be called to sacrifice your life. But if you do not step out into the scary unknown, past the 'zone of comfort' you may never utilize your God-given talents. No, the Christian life is not easy but it can be very exhilarating and rewarding! 'Come and share your master's happiness!' In the end result the risk is only temporary. What is important is that God's love will never be separated from you.

Reflection

Risk is utilizing your God-given talent.
Recklessness is trying to live outside of
God's will.

Prayer

Our gracious heavenly Father, give me an
adventurous heart, that I may
risk all for you.

*'If you want to launch big ships,
you have to go into deep water.'*
JERRY ROOT

*'Expect great things from God,
Attempt great things for God.'*
WILLIAM CAREY

Solutions

Finally, brothers, whatever is true, whatever is noble, whatever is right, whatever is pure, whatever is lovely, whatever is admirable – if anything is excellent or praiseworthy think about such things.'
PHILIPPIANS 4:8

'Whatever you see and believe, you can achieve!' A coach at half-time of a game we were losing corralled us together and yelled repeatedly, 'Whatever you see and believe, you can achieve!' He then made us shout, 'Whatever you see and believe, you can achieve!' He said, 'Say it again, and again! and again!!!'

We took the field with pop-psychology jingles swimming through our head! The coach gave us slogans but no solutions. I recall we went on to lose that game! The trouble with that coach's 'Pep talk' was we could not 'achieve' because we had been given nothing to 'see and believe'. The team wanted to win, but the bridge between winning and seeing was not in place. The work was not done and all we had was useless rhetoric. Thoughts are important, but coaches do not win with slogans which offer no solutions. That coach was fired.

I hate sermons where you are given no solutions. There is very little thought in a thirty-minute sermon where twenty-six minutes describes the problem and four minutes are devoted to the solution. It is quite easy to identify what is wrong in the world. It is easy to point out the world's shortcomings. The difficulty arises in giving people positive solutions. We need to strike at the root of sin. Putting positive bandaids on deep-rooted spiritual pathology never works. A good coach will draw attention to bad technique but a great coach will then show you how to perform. We should not loiter in darkness. A golfer will not improve merely by pointing out a bad swing; he needs to know what a good swing looks and feels like.

Positive improvement comes in internalizing and assimilating good form. The same is true in our spiritual life. We need models of 'good Christian form' in our life. We need to learn from men and women who not only abhor and abstain from gossip, but speak with encouragement.

We need to see people stand for truth and appreciate beauty. We need to see excellence in our churches and purity in thought in Christians. Your job is to find these virtues and 'think about such things', dwell on them. Use your imagination, then model them for others.

Paul is asking us to admire the goodness of the reality in Christ. You may need to look hard to find this 'positive coaching' but it is there. When in doubt, 'fix your eyes on Christ.' We are the sum of our thoughts.

Reflection

Am I dwelling on what is good, pure,
righteous, admirable? Am I an example of
these virtues to others?

Prayer

Lord I want my life to count. Give me your
eternal target and your eternal solutions; and
Help me to press on to your eternal prize.

GIGO: Good In = Good Out

Run for the Prize

Do you not know that in a race all the runners
run, but only one gets the prize? Run in such a way
as to get the prize. Everyone who competes in the
games goes into strict training. They do it to get a
crown that will not last; but we do it to get a crown
that will last forever.'
1 CORINTHIANS 9:24

Here Paul is drawing on his knowledge and understanding of Greek culture in the great city of Corinth. In Paul's time of writing, the population was estimated to have about 650,000 people. Over 400,000 were slaves. Competing in the city's games would have been seen as an escape from the oppressive world of slavery. To win a wreath (medal) in the biannual Isthmian games, the second largest games in Greece, could mean physical emancipation. Performing well in sport could offer you freedom. Paul would have understood the cultural power sport had on the psyche of even the most casual fan in Greece.

The apostle Paul was committed. Paul had a coach's heart: 'strive', 'beat your body', 'look forward', 'Press-on' – these were all major themes in his letters. It was noted by the historian and gospel writer Luke, that Paul was once nearly beaten to death and driven out of a city. Paul, never to be discouraged, got right back up when he had recovered and went back into the city that very night. He was focused and purpose driven. If he was a coach he would expect and get the best out of you. He hated a half-hearted, 'aimless' effort.

Paul takes everyday illustrations and puts them into eternal perspective. Is your goal high enough? Most of us have a yearning for glory, a passion to win. There is an innate longing set in the heart of man to achieve; unfortunately, we often do not aim at eternal achievement, but merely earthly success, which will not satisfy. Paul understood these 'noble desires' couldn't be satisfied with a wooden wreath or a gold medal. Paul gives us the answer, 'Run for the prize that will not perish', live your life with a higher purpose, for a crown that will last forever. The better the sports person you are, the easier it should be to understand that your earthly prizes will not completely satisfy. I know some of you are reading this and saying to yourselves, 'Ah Steve you do not know my goals, if only I could win that prize, play for that team or break that record then I will be happy, then I could sit back and rest on my laurels (trophy).'

I really hope you realize your dream and you make that team or win that prize, then you will understand that although winning is great, the euphoria does not last. It is easier to explain these concepts to champions, than to most who think, 'if only'. Go for the crown that will last forever.

Reflection

Do I keep chasing after things in life that will not make me happy for long?

Prayer

Lord, there is a yearning in my heart, help me to satisfy it.

'He is no fool who gives what he cannot keep to gain what he could never lose.'
JIM ELIOT

Satisfaction

*'May your fountain be blessed, and may you rejoice
in the wife of your youth. A loving doe, a graceful
deer — may her breasts satisfy you always, may
you ever be captivated by her love.'*
Proverbs 5: 18-19

M ost of what is written about sex is for beginners. It is embarrassing to purchase a magazine on fitness, because of the goofy ubiquitous headlines about 'how to have great sex'. I do not want the girl at the counter thinking I need any advice on sex from a magazine hack. I want a fitness magazine to give me tips on weight training, heart rate and nutrition, not on sex. Reading some of those articles one has to laugh, because after fifteen years of marriage most advice for 'great sex' is pretty shallow and novice. Sadly, most of what is written about sex is pretty boring to those in healthy long-term physical relationships. Most articles create unrealistic expectations for youth and people that are outside of a healthy sexual relationship. Most magazine, television and newspaper advice about sex is given by pop-psychology idiots who are desperately trying to meet deadlines. All they do is rehash old myths.

Sex is meant for two people for a lifetime of experience and exploration. Let's put it into perspective, if I gave you 'Ten Great Tips' on how to play a violin, could you play like Vivaldi in a week, or even a year? If that were true then 'Ten Great Tips' on how to play great golf would get you on the pro circuit in a month. Good sex should be seen as a wonderful long-term investment with your spouse.

Sex is such a strong force and so many half-truths surround it. The boundaries are clear, and outside of marriage sexual exploration is dangerous. Sadly, for every Biblical message on sex, you will receive hundreds of messages from the media that will undermine God's great purpose for you sexually.

So why do we not have more clear messages about biblical sexual relationships. First, most Christian literature is written by older people, I believe that they feel they have finally conquered the battle of lust when probably, they have forgotten that their libido has just slowed down. Next, Christian leaders do not want to admit their failures because it is so embarrassing for them, and so many people look up to them. Lastly, there is a multiplicity of scenarios, which makes it hard to give quick answers to the many different issues. Sex is very complex; age and gender create vast differences. For instance, a young male will usually have an almost overwhelming sex drive; they may wonder how one will ever be able to control it and live out the Christian life. A male in middle age may desire the security of still being attractive to the opposite sex. Work out your answers in the light of God's truth, be careful what the media will tell you, remember how God forgives and desires for you to strive for him.

Reflection

Am I being encouraged to live a sexually pure life?

Prayer

Lord that I may be satisfied in you and in your ways.

'The great enemy of the truth is very often not the lie: deliberate, contrived and dishonest; but the myth: persistent persuasive and unrealistic.'
JOHN F. KENNEDY

Shame

'They dress the wound of my people as if it were not serious. "Peace, peace" they say, when there is no peace. Are they ashamed of their loathsome conduct? No, they have no shame at all; they do not even know how to blush.'

JEREMIAH 8:11-12

Have you ever blown it, done something you shouldn't have done or said something you shouldn't have said? You feel your gut wrench and you feel sick inside? Is shame a bad thing? It is a bitter pill to swallow. It is one miserable skin to wear, one I want to rid myself of quickly. But a good definition of shame is: 'an indignity made to restrain a good man from an unworthy act.' If shame, or at least the dread of shame, keeps me from trouble it is no bad thing. Shame, like pain, is a warning to stop, 'Don't go down that road!' Many sporting careers have been cut short by pain killing drugs. Cortisone is a great pain deadener, you still feel the pain but you can play through it. Shame is a very good source of quality control. When we anaesthetise (deaden the pain) shame we live outside the boundaries of our design in the murky world of pseudo-wisdom. Shame helps us to pay allegiance to the truth.

A lack of shame retards creativity. Mind numbing, shamelessness is a slow and subtle seduction which helps us reconcile self-delusion. We start to rationalize and convince ourselves that bad things are okay. Rather than a healthy dose of reality we prefer to dwell in a gloomy fog of shamelessness. Unfortunately, the more calloused we become to shame, our bent for disobedience becomes stronger than our convictions. Shame is a healthy warning that we are in bondage outside God's precincts.

Please beware – shame must never be a weapon of man! Sadly, shame is also a most dangerous form of manipulation. Like chemical warfare it is a cheap and deadly tool in the armoury of hypocrites.

Walk in the light, the pangs of shame that come out of God's truth rid you of the muck that causes spiritual cancer. Shame is not a dwelling place, merely rocket fuel to help us launch out of the mire. Jettison the rubbish and launch to higher realms.

Reflection

Feeling shame is no bad thing, getting used to it is dangerous.

Prayer

'If we claim to be without sin we deceive ourselves and the truth is not in us. If we confess our sins, he is faithful and just and will forgive our sins and purify us from all unrighteousness.'

1 John 1:8-9

'The emotion of shame has been valued not as an emotion but because of the insight to which it leads.'

C. S. LEWIS

Sharing your Faith

When the people heard this, they were cut to the heart and said to Peter and the other apostles, "Brothers what shall we do?"'
ACTS 2: 37

I remember a team-mate coming to me and asking; 'So how do I become a Christian?' After trying to share Christ with this guy for two seasons he was finally open! Here was a great window of opportunity and I choked! My answers were pretty lame!

You may have prayed for your team-mates, encouraged them, given them literature, given them positive role-models, and hopefully shattered their misconceptions of what they perceived a Christian to be – are you prepared for when they ask 'Brothers what shall we do?' Do you have a response? Sometimes we are so focused on preparing the message that when it comes time to deliver, we blow it.

Can you explain the basics of Christianity to a friend or team-mate? The apostle Peter emerged as a brilliant communicator but it wasn't a natural gift. The Holy Spirit had given him the words and he proclaimed them fearlessly. He was prepared. In Acts Chapter 2 we can learn from Peter's very effective proclamation: First, he and his friends had been **praying**. Second, he had **guidance** by the Holy Spirit. Third, he used **scripture** (Joel) to communicate the Good News. Lastly, he was **genuinely eager** for them to be saved (vs. 2: 40 'he pleaded').

Having the opportunity to share your faith with a friend will be one of the most significant opportunities of your life. Be prepared to do your best. Get some training soon, and at the least if you are caught off guard today you can say, 'Let me show you what Peter said when somebody asked him about spiritual matters. Let me show you Acts Chapter 2.'

Reflection

Who can better lead a pro sports person to Christ than another pro. Who could better reach your team-mate than you?

Prayer

Father give me the words and opportunities to tell my team-mates about you.

'Everyday, everyday I have an opportunity to talk to team-mates about my faith.'
DEREK ADAMS, PROFESSIONAL SOCCER PLAYER

Sharing your Faith

'In the same way, let your light so shine before men,
that they may see your good deeds and praise your
Father in heaven.'
MATTHEW 5: 16

You can lead a horse to water but you can't make him drink, but you can put salt in his fodder and make him mighty thirsty.

Real Christianity will make men thirsty. The reason people don't embrace Christ is because it does not seem relevant to them. A recurring theme in the book of Acts is: people are attracted first to Christians – then to Christ. One of the reasons that being a Christian in the world of sport is so effective, is that you are exceptionally exposed. Where else will you get seemingly normal people booing you and making strange gestures at certain parts of your anatomy, and somehow it seems okay! Sport is a roller-coaster of experience, relationships and emotions. It is pretty tough to hide your true self over an entire season. Whether you win or lose everybody seems to notice. You get your face punched in a scrum, you miss a crucial free-throw, you are always asked to be team captain (but not invited to certain parties) and on the team bus your friends scrutinize your reaction to a coarse joke. These events don't happen while you are shopping for potatoes! In the world of sport at any level, whether you like it or not, fans, team-mates and even opponents are watching you.

Sadly most of modern life is lived in compartments and cubicles, but sport is lived in community. This is what our Saviour has asked of you: 'let your light (Jesus) shine before men'. We were called to occupy specific areas of culture for Christ. It is very easy to boycott the ugly parts of society, but Jesus' model was to befriend the sick and the ugly. Your consistency, hard work and humility will shine especially in dark areas of life. You are bound to make mistakes, that's okay. It is your Christian response, after you blow it, which will make an impression. Vital, exciting, robust and joyful faith in Christ, lived-out in your sporting community, will be the best sermon your friends can receive.

Christianity offers solutions. We cannot be seen to be complainers and whiners. We offer the keys to hope and life – 'as one beggar showing another where the food is'! Christ is the intellectual, cultural, social and eternal answer. The more we flesh out the Christian faith and the more we offer positive alternatives to life's problems, the sooner men will embrace and follow Christ. There is plenty of bad news out there, live out the 'Good News'.

One of my pro's invited his team-mate to a ten week Christian discovery course. His team-mate accepted because he saw something different in this guy's life. He was curious – he was thirsty.

Reflection

'True discipleship creates thirst. The reason some men are indifferent to Christianity is that they have never seen it demonstrated.'

RICHARD HALVERSON FORMER CHAPLAIN TO THE U.S. SENATE

Prayer

Holy Spirit, guide my steps,
help me walk in your ways.

'Your talk talks and your walk talks but your walk talks louder than your talk talks.'

FELLOWSHIP OF CHRISTIAN ATHLETES DICTUM

Shut your mouth

'The mouth of the righteous is a fountain of life!'
PROVERBS 10:11

With veins bulging from his temple and eyes popping, the coach screams, 'Referee, you are the dumbest cloth-headed embryo to ever come out of a womb!' The ref. turns to the coach in astonishment and says, 'By golly coach I think you are right! I am the dumbest cloth-headed embryo to ever come out of a womb! I am so grateful for your insight and enlightening me on my shortcomings!' That seems to be an unlikely response. I have asked several referees off the record, 'is screaming at a referee ever advantageous'? **Never!** is the general reply.

I love the sports person who has something to say. They usually are people of few words but when they step-up, the team listens. Words are valuable. In the book of James, chapter 3, the writer likens the tongue to a wild animal needing taming. Like a cowboy trying to tame a wild bronco, Christians need to tame their tongues and master their words. If you are remotely involved with sport, you will be surrounded by foolish words. We must not abdicate our responsibility to be light in darkness, we should not boycott the world of sport, because it is wordly, rather we should occupy the sports world for Christ. But, be cautious, you are being bombarded by unwise language, which is infectious, so ask for God's protection. I had a close Christian friend that kept me and my mouth accountable. During games and practice if I ever let one slip he seemed always to be there. But his 'gentle reproof' was a vicious slap on the back of my neck. I think he enjoyed my accountability, I have a few scars on my neck, but I was cured!

I remember a professor at a Christian University who played soccer for her city team. She played on the team because she wanted to reach her community for Christ. Her one trouble playing on the team was the constant barrage of cursing coming from her team-mates. It would have been far easier for her to stay in the ivory tower of her Christian University, but to her credit she remained with the team, because she loved her team-mates and wanted them to know Christ. One day we were playing soccer together for a church team. She stole the ball and was poised to score; unfortunately, she was tackled from behind. It was a vicious tackle; and, astonishing all, an exceptionally uncharacteristic, unattractive, un-professorial curse spontaneously spewed from her mouth. The poor Prof. had heard so much swearing from her city team that it just came out. She was deeply embarrassed. To her credit her first reaction was to seek forgiveness from her Lord and friends. Only a few self-righteous non-sporty people did not understand. They were probably the ones who went home and gossiped about her.

Reflection

Taming the tongue is a habit of a lifetime,
particularly for those that want to make a
difference in the world of sport.

Prayer

Lord Help me to tame my tongue!

'Wisdom is found on the lips of the discerning...
he who holds his tongue is wise.
The tongue of the righteous is choice silver.
The lips of the righteous nourish many.
The mouth of the righteous brings forth wisdom.
The lips of the righteous know what is fitting.'
PROVERBS 10

'Shut your mouth Connor!'
RUSS GRAHAM

Spiritual Battle

For though we live in the world, we do not wage war as the world does. The weapons we fight with are not the weapons of the world. On the contrary, they have divine power to demolish strongholds.'

2 CORINTHIANS 10:3-4

Whenever I need reminding that we are engaged in spiritual warfare, I put a newspaper and my Bible onto the table. I love my Bible and I love reading newspapers. I look at both and am drawn to the newspaper in a strange kind of way. There is a pull towards the newspaper, something in my mind whispers to me, 'You will find the newspaper more interesting, stay out of the Bible' – almost like a negative divining rod leading me away from water. At this point there is usually a determined effort of the will to draw myself to my Bible.

The Bible is God's truth for us, a compass given by God to nourish, encourage and guide our lives. Thousands of men and women have been martyred so that we can enjoy the freedom of reading the scriptures daily. The Bible is Truth, and has not changed in over two to five thousand years. Yet, when I read from God's word I change, everyday! On the other hand, newspapers change daily. They are full of inaccuracies and interestingly, when I read newspapers, they never change me. A universal supernatural evil, intent on 'devouring you' will do much to try to deceive you and keep you from the power of scripture. Satan does not want to see you walk into battle armed for war.

So lock and load, the spiritual battle is raging. You understand the discipline of sport, the importance of: strict training, pushing yourself hard, rest and making your body conform to your training. These attributes are so valuable to spiritual warfare and to the church. You received a royal inheritance on your awaking to Christ but you also inherited a war. Your determination is needed, but your weapons are far from what you expected. The weapons of God will seem of little use to the ill-informed. When you go into battle you may want to use old fashion out-dated weapons like fist, swords, guns, fighter jets, nuclear weapons or germ warfare. Alternatively, you may want to use wit, logic humiliation, tolerance to lies and ignorance. Your natural instinct to arm yourself with human resources will be of little use. Nevertheless, your arsenal is far more powerful and effective, it includes: universal truth, the power of a pure life, strength of faith and the capability of launching offensives with the Gospel by the Holy Spirit and the most powerful weapon – love! Your commander-in-chief has commissioned you for battle and asks you to employ His weapons. This is a reality with eternal consequences beyond your power to fully comprehend.

Reflection

We do not wage war as the world does.

Prayer

Father I will follow you into this spiritual
battle, but you please lead the way.

*'Haul yourselves up a hundred and one times a day
in order to do it, until you get in the habit of
putting God first and calculating
with Him in view.'*
OSWALD CHAMBERS

Standing Firm

'So then brothers stand firm and hold to the teachings we passed on to you whether by word of mouth or by letter.'
2 THESSALONIANS 2: 15

How encouraging it is to find someone standing firm in his or her faith in the world of sport. It is obvious that some people are drifting spiritually. Many athletes are looking for a new gimmick to improve their performance, so they try Jesus the same way they may try a lucky charm or a new colour of running shoes. Often a superstitious faith is a brand of religion that comes with feigned or half-hearted devotion to God. They do not want to obey their creator; they prefer to have a 'genie in a bottle' that will obey them. When it is convenient, they may go to church or read their Bibles, but they are often merely drifting with the current. Sometimes the drifters get anchored to God and sometimes they flounder and fade away.

An eccentric friend who annoyingly always talks in Christian jargon, asked a colleague of mine, 'When did you wake up?' The colleague was baffled and said, '6:00 am'. My friend was a bit frustrated that he did not catch his line of enquiry and again repeated the question with more emphasis, 'No man, when did you WAKE UP, WAKE UP SPIRITUALLY!!, when did you become a Christian? My colleague was quick and fired back, 'Ah, I woke up in '76, but I did not get out of bed until '80!' There are plenty of Christian weaklings getting pushed around by every new fad or temptation. We need some spiritual tough guys that will not get pushed around and that will hang onto their faith in times of adversity. So get out of bed! Stand firm in your faith, hang on tight to the Word of God, and be a blessing to someone else, someone who has just woken up!

Hebrew 6:19 'We have this hope as an anchor for the soul, firm and secure.'

Reflection
I can stand firm because my feet are on a
secure foundation.

Prayer
Father you are the rock on which I stand.

*'The difference between a successful person and
others is not a lack of strength, but a lack of will.'*
VINCE LOMBARDI

Standing Firm

Finally the temple guards went back to the chief priest, and Pharisees, who asked them, "Why didn't you bring him in?" "No one has ever spoken the way this man does", the guards declared.'
JOHN 7:45-46

S ome people falsely think that the basis of Christianity is eradicating the bad habits in your life. In fact, just the opposite is true, it is filling your life with Christ and letting Him supernaturally draw out the poison. It is a pro-active relationship with Christ, not a boycott of negative habits, that brings restoration.

The temple guards' task was to arrest Jesus for his preaching, but they couldn't do it – it wasn't his time. He was so amazing, so engaging, and so unique that they were dumbfounded. Though they resisted the orders of the Pharisees, who were 'really ticked' by their disobedience, they could not bring themselves to 'bring Him in'. Christ was so different and so compelling that the wrath of their bosses was more inviting than the thought of arresting Jesus.

Behind your back would your friends ever say about you, 'no one has ever spoken like that'. Are you so transformed that you speak more like Christ than you did a year ago? In your speech would friends find graciousness, boldness for truth, and genuine concern for others? Would people say, 'You have been with Jesus'? In contrast to public opinion about professional sportspeople being rough, self-centred egotists, I find my Bible studies with them most encouraging and challenging. There you will find genuine concern for team-mates and their opponents well-being which surpasses many church meetings I go to.

Christ is a world-changer and He wants to enhance your distinctiveness in Him. Christ wants to make you a world changer too. Let God get a hold of you, allow Him to direct your path, pray, 'your will be done', and watch the exciting road you take. Like getting taller, you may not feel the changes taking effect in your life but the more you immerse yourself in Christ the more you will sound and act like Him. The highest complement you may receive could be, 'no one ever spoke the way they spoke!'

Reflection
Is the uniqueness of Christ
rubbing off on me?

Prayer
Dear Lord, continue to permeate my life and
allow me to take on your very nature.

'I must decrease and He must increase.'
JOHN THE BAPTIST ON CHRIST

Training

*'Those who belong to Christ have crucified the
sinful nature with its passions and desires. Since
we live by the Spirit, let us keep in step
with the Spirit.'*
GALATIANS 5:24–25

Again we see Paul using a sporting metaphor, *keep in step*'. In Athletics (Track and Field) training, many sprinters and middle distance runners work-out together. A common training technique is an 'Indian line'. One runner leads and another half dozen sprinters follow in a straight line keeping in pace with the leader. After 300 metres or so the last in the line sprints to the front and sets the new pace. You are caught up in the competition, you do not want to slow down and open-up a gap in the line. It is motivating and fun, you dig deep, push further and challenge each other.

God has you in spiritual training; the Spirit is always pushing you on, challenging you. If you have ever run in a pack you understand the energy of corporate power. Running with others pushes and carries you in a way that you can't get on your own. You are *compelled*.

The same is true in the life controlled by the Spirit; you feel the pace and the power of God. You are running (spiritually) faster and longer than you have before. You can almost hear Christ challenging you, and advancing your Spiritual power, 'Come on, live for Me'. Keeping in step with the Spirit is pure pleasure; you have purpose, direction and encouragement. You know you are in sync with the Lord; you have kept a short account of sin and you are seeking obedience. Life in sync with the Spirit is never stagnant. You are being stretched, you are desiring things that you rarely thought of. The presence of God in your life is as valuable (if not more) as oxygen in your lungs, you now hunger and thirst for righteousness. Keep the pace – 'press on'!

Reflection

Keep in step, push yourself, you know that God will not run ahead of you and leave you in the dust. Enjoy the progress of the spiritual race.

Prayer

Lord Jesus, Thank you that you will help me, guide me and push me. Thank you that I will never take this trip of life on my own.

'Dance then wherever you may be;
I am the Lord of the Dance said he,
And I'll lead you all, wherever you may be,
And I'll lead you all in the dance, said he.'
SYDNEY CARTER

Unity

*'To prepare God's people for works of service, so
that the body of Christ may be built up until we
all reach unity in the faith and in the knowledge of
the Son of God and become mature, attaining to
the whole measure of the fullness of Christ.'*
EPHESIANS 4:12-13

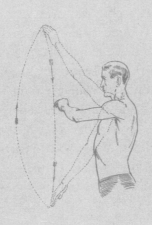

I magine you are on a team where many of the players are jealous of your limited talent. You are learning new moves that they have never seen. You play within the rules but your team-mates have never seen these techniques of yours. The difference in your style makes them feel awkward; all they want you to do is fail. Your team-mates criticize you when you learn new skills and push yourself hard. When you do fail because you are working on improving, they snicker behind your back. Inwardly, they are pleased at your failures. The team feels awkward at your extra work; it makes them feel guilty. I have never played on a team like that, yet I have seen elements of envy on every team I have ever played on; sadly, this includes God's team.

Now imagine being on a team that is so motivated to win that it celebrates your limited talent. Your team-mates watch you and learn new moves from you. You play within the rules but you are looking for every way you can to defeat your opponent. Some of your moves work and because you are trying to succeed some of your plays take on a new technique. The team starts taking on new techniques, even when they are out of their comfort-zones. When you do fail because you are not playing it safe, your team is around you, they pick you up, and push you on because

you have unity and the same sense of purpose.
I have played on teams like this. Happily, even
on God's team.

On a team, good performance and unity
are inseparable.

Which team do you play on?

Reflection
Unity comes with purpose at the cross.

Prayer
Lord help me to encourage unity on my
team, at my work and in my church.

'In essentials – unity.
In non-essentials – liberty.
In all things – Charity.'
RICHARD BAXTER – 1651

'Eunuchs of the world unite –
you have nothing to lose.'

Unity

*We ought always to thank God for you, brothers,
and rightly so, because your faith is growing more
and more, and the love everyone has for
each other is increasing.'*
2 THESSALONIANS 1:3

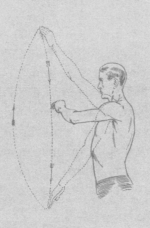

A former Welsh International rugby player went to visit the Samoan team before they went on to play Wales in a championship play-off. Just before the Samoans took the field almost the entire team took a knee and humbled themselves before God in prayer. The Samoans merely prayed that God would be glorified in the competition. The Welsh rugby player who is fiercely patriotic, after seeing the unity of the Samoan players said, 'The Welsh boys have no chance!' He was right, Samoa crushed Wales on the day. A group of people unified around the cross are powerful. When a team plays in sync and the harmony is based on Christ we should thank God. This is happening more and more in the world of sport.

Are you in a body of believers that are thanking God for your 'growing faith'?

When you see a group of Christians that are 'growing in their faith', do you get excited and drawn to thanksgiving? Think of some group that is growing in their faith and thank God for them right now. It may even be your opponents! This exercise will do three things for you; **first**, it will please God for your appreciation of His work in others' lives. **Second**, it will spur you on to desire your own personal growth. **Thirdly**, you will want to be around others that desire that growth and unity.

Take a moment to thank God for a group of believers that are growing in faith. Then ask God for that blessing on your team, Church and community.

Reflection

Desire the best for your team. Their victory
is your victory.

Prayer

Forgive me Lord when I secretly cheer when
a team-mate or fellow Christian fails.

'Unity is strength.'
FRENCH PROVERB

Wake Up!

'And pray in the Spirit on all occasions with all kinds of prayers and requests. With this in mind, be alert and always keep on praying for all the Saints.'
EPHESIANS 6: 18

Out of a jet-lagged slumber I woke to an Arabic chant through an old loud speaker; we were warned by an American couple that the muezzin (one who calls to prayer) would be bellowing 'Wake-up, **wake-up!** It is better to pray than sleep!' The people in the centre of Alexandria, Egypt were not particularly proud of his skill as a chanter, but he woke me from a deep sleep. The first prayer is offered before sunrise, the second in the very early afternoon, the third in the late afternoon, the fourth immediately after sunset, and the fifth before midnight. Whenever I am in a Muslim country I am always struck by the five daily prayers and it encourages me to pray to My Lord and Saviour.

In my daily routine I need a lot of reminders to pray. I hate seeing someone after I promised to pray for them, and then immediately forgot to do it! Why is it that we need to be reminded so much? We are renewable people and need to be refreshed, enriched, nourished, empowered and encouraged all the time. If you do not believe it go without air for one minute and see if you would like a renewal of oxygen. It does not take long to get out of shape physically or spiritually, it takes constant encouragement.

This book is about being spiritually renewed. I hope there will be times in your life when you will say, 'bah! I don't need Connor's book, I can write something better.' Dig through scripture and come up with your own great inspirational ideas. So wake up, get out of bed, it is better to spend time with God than to sleep.

I could not think of a better way to be encouraged than to sit at Jesus' feet, spend some time with Him and learn.

Reflection
When your batteries are low, you must be
alert for the enemy will attack.

Prayer
Lord again and again and again remind me to
worship you.

'What we remember is what we become.'
JOHN OSBORNE

Wearing the Uniform

*'Quick bring the best robe and put it on him. Put a
ring on his finger and the sandals on his feet.
Bring the fatted calf and kill it. Let's have a feast
and celebrate. For this son of mine was dead and
now is alive again.'*
LUKE 15: 22-24

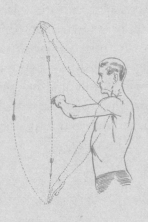

Do you remember receiving your first sports uniform? I didn't want to take mine off and probably wore it to bed! There is something about humans that loves definition, and validation. One of the great things about sport is that it sets margins. You're either part of the team or you're not. You win or lose. You have a low handicap or a high one. We enjoy being part of a group. The more others want to be part of a group the more esteemed the group is. Even anti-group types form their own counter-cultures and wear anti-social clothing (which is just another uniform), jewellry, haircuts... Ironically the anti-establishment uniform usually becomes the next generation's establishment kit. At one time not wearing a tie to watch a sporting event was considered socially outrageous!

Being adopted into God's family gives you certain rights, privileges and responsibilities.

You wear a new uniform. If you are a Christian you have been adopted into God's family. You are now a princess or a prince. You belong to God and you have a new allegiance, a new title and new citizenship. And, like enjoying being part of a team, you also have new duties and responsibilities that come with the uniform.

'So you are no longer a slave, but a son; and since you are a son, God has made you also an heir.' Galatians 4:7

Reflection

Being on God's Team gives us certain
privileges and certain responsibilities.

Prayer

Lord help me to act like your ambassador
and your son.

*'If you are a true Christian, then you are a
minister. A non-ministering Christian is a
contradiction in terms.'*
ELTON TRUEBLOOD

When the Odds Are Against You

*'And an evil spirit said to them, "I recognize Jesus,
and I know Paul, but who are you?" And the man
in whom was the evil Spirit, leaped on them and
subdued all of them, and overpowered them, so
that they fled out of the house naked and
wounded... and the name of the Lord Jesus was
being magnified.'*
ACTS 19: 15–17

The scene reminds me of a martial arts film, seven brothers of a Jewish chief priest who dabble in exorcism. The brothers heard of the supernatural power that comes in Christ's name, the boys could not wait to try out this new power. Encountering a man with an evil spirit they tried to cast it out of him in Jesus' name. The spirit responded, 'I know Jesus – but who are you!' The evil spirit went on to beat the boys so badly that they ran from the house naked and wounded. That must have been a bad whipping! What a mistake to use Christ's name so casually – it really backfired on these pretenders.

We can learn from this scene. First, we must be fully devoted to Christ to have effective power. Do not dabble with faith in Christ. To be a useful Christian you need to be fully committed to Him. Many play at their faith without really understanding the spiritual danger they are in.

Be aware of the spiritual battle we live in and stay close to Christ's protection.

Next, understand the spiritual power you have in Christ when you are committed to Him. Do you appreciate that there is power in the name of Jesus? I find that the quickest way to get at the core of any religious debate is to simply ask, 'What do you think and feel about Jesus?' Most of the time people will try to avoid the question because some strange spiritual warfare has begun to be waged in their soul. Quickly, the subject is diverted to 'religion' or the evils of religious wars. Bring them back to Jesus. He is perfect and powerful. There will be times when you feel that you are making no impact at all with your team mates or in the office or at school. There will be seasons in your life when the achievements you so desperately desired don't come in the way you plan. Search your scriptures and you will never see that the follower of Christ is exempt from pain, frustration and loneliness. But you are promised power, guidance and a commitment from God that you need never walk alone. You can walk through life thinking the odds are stacked against you, never realizing the spiritual safety and power you have in Christ.

Reflection

Remember: one demon-possessed man
against seven uncommitted brothers were
bad odds for the boys. Stay in His power
and give yourselves fully to Christ.

Prayer

Lord Jesus take your place in my heart and
lead me into life.

*'When Jesus is with us, all is well,
and nothing seems difficult.'*
THOMAS À KEMPIS

FINISHING WELL

'I have fought the good fight, I have finished the race, I have kept the faith. Now there is in store for me the crown of righteousness, which the Lord, the righteous Judge, will award to me on that day — and not only to me, but also to all who have longed for his appearing.'
2 TIMOTHY 4:7-8

Transformation

*'But our citizenship is in heaven. And we eagerly
await a Saviour from there, the Lord Jesus Christ,
who, by the power that enables him to bring
everything under his control, will transform our
lowly bodies so that we will be like his
glorious body.'*
PHILIPPIANS 3:20-21

This is a devotional for people who want to progress.

I saw my old coach whom I love and respect last month and he seemed even closer to Christ and his faith more vibrant than the last time I saw him. He is sixty-seven and still has a deep desire to be transformed into the likeness of Christ. It gives me great optimism. My old coach will never change, for him to change would be to stop moving forward, to stop desiring God. He knows he is on a journey, he knows where his citizenship rests.

Do you grasp how hard it is and yet, how fundamental it is to progress? Your brain, your body and even your friends resist your transformation. Habit, routine and a planned agenda give a sense of security. The older you get, the harder change becomes. It is much easier to transplant a sapling than a mature tree.

Here is a suggestion: orientate your life so you always progress. Recognize you are on a lifetime development. Pilgrims do not stop until they reach their destination. If you walk with God from an early age, you will understand that God will challenge you. Have you been challenged lately? He desires you to transform, to metamorphose. You are a butterfly in progress. For a young person to progress with God is normal. An older

Christian is still on the journey. The progression finishes when your heart stops beating, not before.

Make it a habit to put God at the centre of your routine and your security will be in the eternal, your finishing line is nothing short of Heaven's gates.

Reflection

Our spiritual training is to last a lifetime,
it is a long season.

Prayer

Gracious Father I pray that I don't get stuck
in a rut. I want to have a lifetime of
adventure following you.

*'If I find in myself a desire which no experience in
this world can satisfy, the most probable
explanation is that I was made for another world.'*
C.S. LEWIS *Mere Christianity*

Trophies

'What do these stones mean?'
JOSHUA 4:6

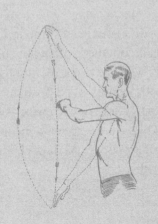

A friend of mine keeps his national, continental, commonwealth and Olympic medals at the bottom of his fish tank! Whenever I see them among the fish, I grin. The medals are a reminder of his wonderful achievements, and the perspective he gives them. The Old Testament character, Joshua, was Moses' anchorman! He was passed the baton from the massive figure of Moses and told to finish the race God set out for the Israelites, to cross the Jordan River into the Promised Land. This particular race lasted forty years! However, humans have a bad memory. Even though a great miracle occurred at the beginning of the race (the famous crossing of the Red Sea); and even though God sustained the Israelites with food from heaven, the Israelites seemed forever in fear. Forgetting about God's miraculous and constant provision, the Israelites were always hankering after their times of slavery back in Egypt.

God works in our lives, sometimes his work is extravagant, but more often it is subtle. God also knows we have short memories. For this reason God commanded Joshua to pile up twelve stones – one for each tribe – at the river Jordan. This was a special monument to remind God's people and their children, what He did for them.

My son was so pleased to discover hiding behind his bed a certificate he was awarded the previous year when he was three years old. The certificate brought back distant memories of some distinguished honour (tying his shoes) he received a quarter of his life ago! We also have short memories and need memory stones, memorials marked for us. You may have trophies and medals in places of honour in your house, you may have them collecting dust in your attic. How many memory stones do you have of God working in your life? Remember the miracle of first opening your life to Christ! Do you recall the very real presence you felt from Christ during a certain personal disaster. Do you remember when a particular scripture verse seemed to be written just for you? Remember that special prayer request that was answered early on in your walk with Him?

Write these things down. Etch them with indelible ink into your memory. When the winds blow and the rain comes remember God is there and ask him to remind you – 'What do these stones mean?'

Reflection

We can't live in the past, but we all need to be reminded of God's power. During the 'valley times' in your life you need to cast your memory back to when God blessed you in some special way.

Prayer

Father I remember when you did
_____in my life. Thank you.

'Be strong and courageous.'
GOD

Victory

*'So it will be with the resurrection of the dead.
The body that is sown is perishable, it is raised
imperishable… The sting of death is the sin, and
the power of sin is the law. But thanks be to God
he gives us victory through our Lord Jesus Christ.'*
1 CORINTHIANS 15:42, 56-57

In a village in central Scotland lies an old cramped graveyard. It was burgeoning with bones and couldn't hold one more body. After much debate, anxiety and committee meetings the good folks in the village finally agreed to a cemetery extension in the field next to the old gravesite. The trees were cut down, the grass was sown and then the whole village waited and watched. Who would be the first to use the new field? It seemed a pity, almost a snub, but no one was coming forward to oblige the committee's hard work, no one wanted to try out the new burial ground! The field lay empty for quite a long time. It was a strange sight, to the right was a graveyard that looked quaint, old and heaving with gravestones; to the left, divided by a stonewall was a sterile, immaculately cut, empty field. Who would have the honour of trying out the new extension?

Then it happened that some old unassuming dear who had never won anything in her life is now famous for being the first to try out the new turf. The entire village was quite proud of her undertaking this 'ground breaking' achievement. Then it all seemed horrible. The village's novel pride of the lady's feat, changed to a sense of sadness. Seeing the poor lady interned all alone in that vast empty field was gloomy. So now the village wanted someone to go and keep her company! Again the village waits.

Another old Scot George MacDonald once wrote, 'Your mother teaches you wrongly when she says, you are a body and have a soul, for you are soul and have a body.' It is good to remember that we are not really bodies but souls. I have an old jersey I keep in a cedar chest, it reminds me of a special team I played for and it represents a special time in my life. The jersey has good memories but it is not me, unless I choose to live in the past. A grave is like that, the cast-off jar of clay represents memories good and bad but if I live in the past , I live in the grave. We can stand firm, look forward and know our victory in Christ will last for eternity.

Reflection

In the broader sense – on God's Team we already know the outcome.

Prayer

Dear Father in Heaven, we remember that our 'Victory' cost you much.

'I have never won a victory that compared to being on God's Championship Team.'
COACH REX

Well Done

'As a father has compassion on his children, so the Lord has compassion on those who fear him...'
PSALM 103:13

Once, at a high school sporting match; I asked the couple sitting next to me if they would point out their son, as I would love to watch him play. They were surprised and caught a little off-guard – it was odd to me that they appeared to care so little about the game. Then they realized I had assumed they were there to watch their son compete. The couple laughed and explained apologetically, that they were not much interested in the game. 'We are looking forward to half-time so we can enjoy our son perform in the schools marching band'.

Sure enough half-time came and when most of the crowd were busy buying refreshments and discussing the game, the parents next to me seemed to wake up and fix their attention on the field (pitch). They were animated and proud to point out their son; a little chubby fellow blowing relentlessly on the biggest tuba I had ever seen. His effort seemed magnificent as I watched it through the eyes of his parents. Then his mother in tense posture announced, 'this is the tough part, here he goes', then she exclaimed, 'oh he missed a note' as she put her face into her husband's chest. But soon the mother again cheered as he evidently performed the right note in a difficult measure. You can put all I know about music in a thimble, and still have room for your thumb. I was amazed that she could tell from where she stood what he was about to play. Another tough musical medley came and ,he, clearly, from his mother's reaction, played his part perfectly. The boy's parents were certainly enjoying themselves judging by their look of pleasure and satisfaction. Tuba-boy and the rest of the band eventually marched off the pitch and on came the teams. Funnily, Tuba-boy's parents gathered their things and politely said goodbye, preferring to get home rather than finishing the game.

We often think of God as one who only gets involved when we are having fun and wants to ruin it for us. Being a father (a rather poor one compared to my Heavenly father), I realize it is just the opposite. I love to hear my children laugh and I love to watch them perform. They 'blow notes' all the time and because I want them to live life to the full, I try to instruct them. Our Heavenly father is the same. He is interested in all you are doing, He wants you to do your best. I can almost hear him pointing out to some angel, 'Hey there is my boy, look, look there's my girl, this is a tough part, YA THEY DID IT! WELL DONE!'

Reflection

When I became a Father I realized the patience and love our Heavenly Father has for us. Our spiritual journey will some day finish, our ultimate praise will be from our Father – Well Done!

Prayer

Lord, guide me to victory.

'Hey bro, it aint just about starting well, its about finishing well.'
JACK VANDIVER

SCRIPTURE INDEX

Christian Focus Publications publishes biblically accurate books for adults and children. The books in the adult range are published in three imprints.

Christian Heritage contains classic writings from the past.

Christian Focus contains popular works including biographies, commentaries, doctrine, and Christian living.

Mentor focuses on books written at a level suitable for Bible College and seminary students, pastors, and others; the imprint includes commentaries, doctrinal studies, examination of current issues, and church history.

For a free catalogue of all our titles,
please write to:

Christian Focus Publications, Ltd.
Geanies House, Fearn, Tain,
Ross-shire, IV20 1TW, Great Britain

For details of our titles visit us on our website:

http://www.christianfocus.com